W9-DAN-147

Praise for:

Treasure Hunt

"*Treasure Hunt* provides some well-worth-your-consideration guidance for today's emerging success seekers. Rather than looking at achieving success through the old maxims of yesterday's business models, the author, Rizwan Virk, shows us how the latest thinking based on quantum physics and specifically the multiverse/parallel universes models, provides you with new maps of understanding that can guide you to getting what you want navigating through today's jungle of multiple opportunities and dense misadventures."

Fred Alan Wolf PhD, aka Dr. Quantum®, author of *Parallel Universes,* and *Dr. Quantum Presents: Do-it-Yourself Time Travel*

"The world around us is speaking to us every day in a language of signs and symbols, if only we pay attention. Riz Virk is an active student of synchronicity. He invites us to look at the patterns of everyday life as a treasure map, offering clues we can follow to manifest our life dreams. Charmingly, he urges us to bring the spirit of Indiana Jones to our daily treasure hunt, and animates his 'book of clues' with lively and instructive personal tales"

Robert Moss, bestselling author of *Conscious Dreaming, The Secret History of Dreaming* and *Sidewalk Oracles: Playing with Signs, Symbols and Synchronicity in Everyday Life*

"Riz Virk has made an important contribution to understanding how real success happens. It is more than luck, hard work and brains— an intuitive and consciousness component distinguishes the ordinary from the truly great. As an emergency and trauma MD, I have had many cases where my 'gut' instincts, or intuition, made the difference between life and death. It turns out, this deeper aspect of mind or consciousness is always operating, and we can train ourselves to connect to this inner knowing voice. Everyone can enhance their lives and their careers by understanding what Riz Virk explains in this important new book."

Steven M. Greer MD, SiriusDisclosure.com, author of *Unacknowledged*

"In *Treasure Hunt*, Riz Virk journeys through interpretations of quantum physics and ancient philosophical traditions from various cultures to provide the modern entrepreneur a unique multi-dimensional blueprint for success, with practical clues to help one achieve the best possible future."

Dr. Anita Goel, Chairman and CEO, Nanobiosym and Harvard—MIT physicist and physician and XPRIZE winner

"I can't tell you how excited I am about *Treasure Hunt*! It reveals 'the other side of the story' when it comes to business and personal fulfillment: awakening to your inner guide and following the clues to success. It's a magical book. You will love it."

Adam Curry, founder of *Entangled*, researcher from Princeton's PEAR Lab

"*Treasure Hunt* introduces us to synchronicities—those calling cards from the universe, dropped upon the desk of everyday life, which can change our course in an instant. Virk shows us that our inner compass is a source of great energy and power, and provides a creative toolset to harness this power moment by moment. Strongly recommended for all those who wish to experience the miracles of being *in the flow*."

Dr. Ji Hyang Padma, Director, Comparative Religion & Philosophy, California Institute for Human Science (CIHS) and author of *Living the Season: Zen Practice for Transformative Times*

"*Treasure Hunt* reminds us of the magic in the world—that there are clues happening around us all the time—if we stay awake enough to notice them and then follow them. Riz does not just entertain: he awakens us!"

Lorin Beller, Spiritual/Business Coach and Strategist

...And praise for:

Zen Entrepreneurship: Walking the Path of the Career Warrior

"*Tales of Power* meets the *Peaceful Warrior* ... in Silicon Valley!
It's entertaining, humble, insightful and valuable—not just to
entrepreneurs, but to anyone looking to manifest their dreams and
make a difference in the world."
    Foster Gamble, Creator and Host, *Thrive: What on Earth Will It Take*

"Riz Virk brings the wisdom of ancient Eastern traditions into a
purely Western setting. The result is an often hilarious but always
insightful book that will change how you view career success and
help you discover and walk your own unique path."
    Marc Allen, author of *Visionary Business*, CEO and co-founder of
New World Library

"*Zen Entrepreneurship* changed my life, it confirmed for me that
'clues' exist in the world around us and are powerful. I shared this
book with every one of my clients from that point forward. Powerful.
A must read ... it reinforces that there is a bigger guide within us if
we choose to listen."
    Lorin Beller, author of *From Entrepreneur to Big Fish: 7 Principles
of Wild Success*

"You will come away with insight about yourself, guidance ... and
knowledge that you may not be able to acquire anywhere else save
the mountaintops of the Himalayas."
    Bookreview.com

"I intuitively know this book will be one I read over and over
throughout different times in my life, and each time I suspect I'll
learn even more new and invaluable lessons. *Zen Entrepreneurship*
is a must-have for any spiritual library."
    Chris Cade, spiritual-short-stories.com

For Ellen

who followed the clues with me

TREASURE HUNT

Follow Your Inner Clues to Find True Success

Rizwan Virk

WATKINS

Sharing Wisdom Since
1893

This edition first published in the UK and U.S.A. 2017 by
Watkins, an imprint of Watkins Media Limited
19 Cecil Court, London WC2N 4EZ

enquiries@watkinspublishing.com

1 3 5 7 9 10 8 6 4 2

Designed and typeset by Clare Thorpe

Printed in Great Britain by CPI Group (UK) Ltd, Croydon CR0 4YY
A CIP record for this book is available from the British Library

ISBN: 978-1-78678-050-8

www.watkinspublishing.com

Contents

"Your time is limited, so don't waste it living someone else's life. Don't be trapped by dogma—which is living with the results of other people's thinking.

Don't let the noise of others' opinions drown out your own inner voice. And most important, have the courage to follow your heart and intuition. They somehow already know what you truly want to become. Everything else is secondary."

–Steve Jobs
CEO of Apple Computer and Pixar,
Stanford Commencement Ceremony

PART I

THE CLUES

CHAPTER 1

Follow the Clues
to Find the Treasure

Overview

When I was a kid, I was a big fan of adventure films like *Raiders of the Lost Ark*, where the legendary archaeologist, Indiana Jones (played by Harrison Ford), sets out with his friends to find the treasure. It didn't matter whether it was the Ark of the Covenant or the Holy Grail or some other random treasure—it was exciting to watch the twists and turns that led our heroes to the treasure.

For those who are younger, you might recall a similar thrill in watching Benjamin Franklin Gates (played by Nicolas Cage) set out with a clue written on the back of the Declaration of Independence to find the Treasure of the Ages in the film *National Treasure*.

The problem, for all of these heroes, was that although there was a treasure, the map to find it wasn't presented all at once . . . there would be one clue, and only by following that clue could the *next* one be discovered. Sometimes, our heroes would encounter obstacles ranging from Nazi soldiers to new construction over old historic sites, which would prevent them from finding the next clue. Sometimes they would be led down a false path and would have to backtrack to get back on the right trail.

As a kid, simply drawing a Treasure Map could turn an ordinary backyard into a magical adventure. I would suddenly imagine that I was Indiana Jones, following the clues to find a treasure that was hidden long ago by pirates, wizards, or other magical beings.

As we grow up, we lose this sense of adventure and wonder in our daily lives as we settle into the routine of our jobs, our families and our careers. Treasure hunts, we tell ourselves, are for kids. In the real world, we have mortgages, car payments, bills to pay, and don't have time for such "flights of fancy."

What if you could bring back some of the magic and sense of adventure of those classic treasure hunts into your life and career today? Would it lead you to be more passionate, more engaged in your job, or to a more satisfying career? Would it lead you to be more successful?

The Real Treasure: Finding True Success

This book is about turning your career and your life into your own personal treasure hunt so that you can find your own personal definition of *true success*.

Have you ever felt that you were meant to be more successful, more fulfilled and more challenged by your work? If so, you are not alone. Many of us have a sneaking feeling that we were meant to do and accomplish more in this life. It's as if we have some "work" we were *meant* be successful at, based on our own internal strengths; if only we could find it and support ourselves along the way, then all would be well.

The scenario that this book wants you to consider is this: what if there was a Treasure Map that had already been drawn for you, before you entered this life, and all you had to do was follow the clues to find the treasure?

What would be this treasure in your life?

• Would it be starting a successful company and selling it for millions of dollars?

• Would it be writing that novel you have always dreamed of?

- Or would it be writing a book about your life lessons and getting it published?
- Would it be helping others through counseling or therapy or working as part of a charity?
- Would it be indulging your passion as a photographer or as an artist?
- Would it be writing a screenplay for a major Hollywood movie?

True success, the treasure that your personal Treasure Map is pointing to, can come in many forms. For the purpose of this book, it is defined as being in the *right* place at the *right* time, doing *work* that you find *meaningful*, and being *successful* at it.

My friend Dannion Brinkley, who went through a famous near-death experience after being struck by lightning, described in his bestseller, *Saved by the Light*, refers to "Spiritual Capitalism" as an environment in which everyone is contributing to society and able to make a living, leveraging their natural strengths rather than simply "getting by" doing something uninspiring.

For many of us, these scenarios might be great dreams, but we don't know quite how to turn them into reality. We've all read the books about visualization and the law of attraction, but they don't always seem to get us there. Or, for some of us, we might not know what *true success* looks like, but we have a vague sense of our strengths and weaknesses, and don't doubt that we can contribute in some way.

Follow the Clues to Find the Treasure

If only we had the Treasure Map laid out clearly in front of us, we could follow the clues to find the treasure of *true success*, just like Indiana Jones.

What if, because you couldn't see the Treasure Map all at once, you had to find the clues one by one? What might help would be a wise old mentor who could tell you where to go next in your career or your life—an Obi-Wan Kenobi or Gandalf-type figure who could not only offer specific advice on handling day-to-day business decisions, but more importantly, guide you to the people and places that would make a difference in your career long term?

This book was written to tell you that there is a Treasure Map, and that we already have a wise old mentor, inside of us (our "inner mentor"), who is constantly sending us *clues*. Our challenge is to learn to recognize these clues for what they are.

These clues come to us in the form of personalized messages: synchronicity, hunches, gut feelings, visions, feelings of *déjà vu*, bodily sensations, and even in our dreams while we are asleep. These clues offer us guidance, as though we have our own personal GPS, to get back on track in the treasure hunt of our lives and our career, but unfortunately we usually don't recognize them, or if we do, we don't act on them.

Cultures and traditions ranging from Native American tribes to Greek, Roman, Tibetan, Chinese and Islamic have recognized this fundamental truth, but in the modern world of science and technology, we have lost the ability to see these clues, and to have the confidence to follow them. We have lost our inner guides and our compasses are attuned to the wrong criteria.

These clues almost always involve tuning into some internal feeling that is sparked by some external stimulus in the world around us. A *synchronicity*, a term coined by Carl Jung, is the perfect type of clue, because it involves both an internal feeling/sensation, and a co-relation with an external event. The simplest example would be that you think of a friend you haven't thought of in a long time, and they call you the next day. By generalizing this idea to include many types of internal and external clues, this book teaches us how to *recognize* and *follow* the clues.

As in any good mystery or Indiana Jones film, if you follow the clues, you can find the treasure. However, there will be obstacles along the way. In addition to our own thick-headedness in not recognizing the clues, our personal patterns can be either helpful or hurtful in our personal treasure hunt. In this book, we'll explore both "clues" and "anti-clues," the real-world equivalent of the obstacles in the adventure-film versions of treasure hunts.

In this book, you will read about many successful businessmen and women, ranging from entrepreneurs to managers in the corporate world, from artists to professors, who inhabit places as diverse as Silicon Valley to Hollywood to Academia to Wall Street. Moreover, you'll see examples from ordinary people who are not famous but have learned to listen to their intuition and recognize the power of *synchronicity* at work in their lives and in their career, not as a one-off but as a way of navigating and succeeding in the business world.

Most successful entrepreneurs, executives, investors, movie stars and producers use their intuition regularly—in the form of "gut feelings" and "hunches" about clients, employees, investors, screenplays, even while evaluating new business opportunities. The right intuition, if acted upon, can help us find our ideal career path, our next big product idea to leapfrog our competitors, even provide inspiration for creative endeavors that can lead to wealth and fame, or more importantly, to our own personal treasure, your version of *true success*.

CASE STUDY NO. 1:

A Fiery Vision

Let's start with a very vivid example of a *clue* that came in the form of a dream.

James was a young aspiring filmmaker seeking his fortune in the movie industry. He started by helping to create cheap props and effects on the set of not very well-known B-movies. One night, while working on a project in Rome in 1981, he became ill and had to retire and spend several days in bed.

That first night, he had a particularly terrifying dream vision—it was so vivid and troubling that he got up in the middle of the night and drew a picture of what he had seen. In this dream vision, he saw robots emerging from the fire after an apocalypse of some kind. In the dream, a robot was coming to kill him. For the next few days, he couldn't get this vision out of his mind and he showed the picture to his friend, Gail, who also was just starting out and had experience in helping with B-movies.

She encouraged him to turn the picture into an actual script for a movie, which he eventually did. It took many twists and turns before the movie was finally made on a very small budget; in fact, his experience in using cheap props to achieve on-screen effects proved crucial in getting the movie done.

While this back-story may not be familiar to you, you are most likely familiar with the movie, *The Terminator*, which went on to become one of the biggest and most successful movies of 1984, and its director, James Cameron. That original clue led to the film that launched the career not only of Cameron, but also of his friend, producer Gail Ann Heard, and, oh yeah, it turned a bodybuilder who was not a very well-respected actor, Arnold Schwarzenegger, into a superstar.

This kind of dream is what we call a *Big Clue*, in the form of a *Big Dream* for James Cameron, which impacted his life and career profoundly—not only did the success of the movie propel him into the A list of Hollywood directors, but it also set the stage for his subsequent financial success.

James Cameron is only one of many successful people whose intuition provided very important clues about their future. These clues didn't come completely out of the blue—in this case he was already involved in making movies, for example. But it was a synthesis of information and creative inspiration to form a new story.

By following the clues that our intuition gives us, sometimes in big visions and dreams, and sometimes in little hunches, many individuals have been able to follow a path toward career success. As is the case with the Terminator, you may have heard about their success, but you may not know the role that *intuition* played in getting them there.

The Many Types of Clues

Intuition can come in many forms, from a "hunch" while you are waiting in line at the grocery store, a "tingle" at the edge of your awareness about a book on the shelf in a bookstore, a "little voice" that tells you that something is wrong with a plan that a colleague is trying to sell you on, or a full-blown vision that comes to you in the middle of the night in the form of a dream that reveals your next step in life.

Each of these types of intuition is a "clue," and somewhere in your subconscious you have an inner mentor who is hard at work sending you these clues all the time. The clues are often subjective—they are specific to each of us, and if we learn to listen, they can have a profound impact on our lives.

Learning to listen to these clues is like having your own inner mentor who uses an "invisible hand" to point you in a direction that leads to a new job, a new relationship, a new work of art, a new business, or shows you how to improve what you are already doing.

A quick preview of the types of clues you will learn to recognize and act on in this book will include:

- **Hunches.** A hunch is a feeling that we get about someone or something—this could be about a candidate for a job at work, a person we meet on the street, or a company we drive by. We all have hunches, though they come to us in different forms. A hunch, like a famous quote about pornography, is difficult to define but "you'll know it when you see it."

- **Synchronicity and coincidences.** First termed by Carl Jung, a synchronicity is a "meaningful coincidence," often an event in the external world, which *coincides* with some internal thought we have been having. A synchronicity is a clue of the highest order, a "glitch" in the matrix of the world around us that can help to reveal a larger pattern at work in our lives that we may not be able to see consciously.

- **Big Dreams.** Dreams have been a favorite way for our intuition to communicate with us since we were tribes of hunter/gatherers. Not only shamans, but also scientists, businessmen, politicians and religious leaders throughout history have used dreams as a way to find the best solution to a problem, avoid a threat, or receive inspiration for a new work of art or business. We will see many stories about how dreams can be used to achieve career success, and several chapters are devoted to using dreams and waking visions as a way to tune in and recognize when a "big" or "little" dream is pulling you in a certain direction.

- **Sense of certainty.** Sometimes we see a name or person or hear about a place for the first time and we are certain that we have to meet them, or we have to go to a particular place. This is a special type of clue, and we will see numerous case studies of how to recognize and test it, in our case studies.

- **The little voice.** Sometimes we have a little voice that is telling us not to do something, or warning us about some course of action. With all of the mental chatter and pressure to conform, particularly inside big companies, we can drown out the little voice.
- *Déjà vu* **and uncanny feelings.** Sometimes we see an external event or person and have a "funny" or "uncanny feeling" about them, or a sense of *déjà vu* that we have seen the person or the place before. Learning to pay attention to these "funny feelings" is a key step in learning to recognize the clues on your own personal treasure hunt.
- **Internal sensations.** Most messages from our inner mentor come to us with a form of bodily sensation. A tightening up when we hear about a certain company or person, a feeling of joy when we think about ourselves going down a particular path, or the "funny feeling" or sense of "*déjà vu.*" Many of the chapters in this book are devoted to learning how your own body reacts when a clue or an "anti-clue" is being revealed. In some sense this type of clue underlies all the other types.

CASE STUDY NO. 2:
What's in a Name?

Let's take a less dramatic, but perhaps more illustrative example from my own career as an entrepreneur. I had started a company in Cambridge, Massachusetts, which was building products related to a new technology called XML (the idea itself came to me in a dream—but we'll talk more about this later).

My co-founders and I couldn't decide on what to name our start-up, so we gave it a generic placeholder name, XYZ Technologies.

None of us liked this name, and this topic was on my mind as I went home to visit my parents in Michigan for a Christmas vacation. During that vacation, I had reason to visit a friend in Ann Arbor, home to the University of Michigan. As I drove back on the freeway on a relatively cold but sunny winter day, my eyes were drawn to a two-story office park on the side of Interstate 94.

Now, I had driven this road many times before, but I had not noticed this specific building or the name of a company that was on the side of the building. The name of the company was "Arbortext." I had that funny feeling that there was something important about this company or perhaps its name, but I wasn't sure what. As I went home, I kept this "funny feeling" in the back of my mind.

This is usually how *clues* come to us in daily life, in the form of "funny feelings" that stay with us. Sometimes it's obvious what the clue is telling us—but often, we need to go back and "interpret" the clue before taking action.

After I flew back to Boston, I recalled the company name and the funny feeling I'd been having about it. I did some research on the company and realized they were a pioneer in the field of XML and structured documentation, providing tools for some of the biggest pharmaceutical and manufacturing companies in the world (including Boeing and Toyota, etc.).

Then it hit me! Here was an XML-related start-up

located in the college town of Ann Arbor, started by a few alumni of the University of Michigan, which had named itself Arbortext. We were an XML-related start-up located in another college town, Cambridge, started by a couple of MIT alums.

Why not call our company "CambridgeText"?

This seemed like a good solution to our dilemma, as we all liked the name and the association with both our alma mater and the start-up environment around Cambridge. As we were about to finalize the name, I thought it might sound a little too much like Arbortext, so we decided to change it to "CambridgeDocs," short for Documents, which fitted our target market just as well.

This was a case where a funny feeling about something that the "invisible hand" pointed out in the external environment was an answer to a question I had been turning over in my mind internally for weeks.

One Clue Leads to Another . . . over Time

So, we had solved our immediate concern about our name. But the best clues usually indicate not just one answer, but also an overall direction to follow. Clues have many stages and are reflected back to us if we are open to that as part of a larger pattern in our lives and our work.

As I reflected on the name, I began to think more about this company, Arbortext. It was only natural that we would eventually encounter them, because they were one of the better-established players in the technology area we were dealing with.

The clue helped to shortcut the process. I decided to

email one of the founders listed on the website, told them that I was from Michigan originally and indicated that I wanted to explore a partnership. Several months later, when I was visiting my parents again, I went in to meet with one of their senior technology guys, and showed him the product we were building. He was impressed with the product, but told me they had their own internal tool to do what our product did, which was to migrate legacy documents into XML. So, they would keep us in mind, but there wasn't an immediate opportunity for a partnership. I left the meeting with another funny feeling.

Normally, if I wanted to explore a partnership with someone or sell them on our product and the immediate answer was "no," I would feel a little down after the meeting. But I found myself leaving this meeting feeling rather elated, with a different type of clue, a "funny feeling" that said that something would come of the meeting.

You'll find throughout this book that "clues" sometimes indicate direction, and sometimes indicate timing, but rarely does one clue indicate both. Too often, we read stories about "visualization" and "synchronicity" that sound amazing, but when our first few clues seem to lead to a dead end, we can get discouraged. Don't let that happen. Remember, if finding the treasure were easy, there wouldn't be much point in the treasure hunt!

We went on with our business, and about a year later, I got an email from someone at Arbortext saying that I had made a good impression on their VP, and that they were looking to have a new tool to convert documents to XML.

In this case, they wanted to explore a partnership, which

we worked on. To make a long story short, they became our biggest customer and they introduced our product into some of the biggest manufacturing companies in the world, giving us instant credibility and making us an acknowledged leader in our market space.

Of course this process took many more months, and required involving both the Right Brain (following intuition) and the Left Brain (following logic and explaining the business case).

The Clue Lifecycle: Bringing Right Brain and Left Brain Together

Science tells us that while the Right Brain is great at intuition, the Left Brain is more practical and logical. This book introduces the *Clue Lifecycle*, a framework which will help you get beyond the usual tropes of "follow your intuition" and "visualize success" to bring the Right Brain and Left Brain together into harmony, in a new way to navigate in your career and the business world.

To be successful in the real world requires not just intuition, but also right action and right timing. If you have a vision of being a painter in Italy, for example, should you quit your job on day one and buy a plane ticket to Italy?

While other self-help gurus might say yes, *Treasure Hunt* is about being both practical and successful on your unique life path. In this book, we'll explore when to follow a clue and when you shouldn't follow one.

In Chapter 2, "The Book of Clues," we'll explore a way for you to start accumulating your own personal clues to find your own treasure. We'll also start to explore the *Rules of Treasure Hunting,* which will be revealed throughout the book to guide us in recognizing clues in the world around us.

In Chapter 3, "The Clue Lifecycle: How to Navigate," we'll introduce a framework and an informal process that can bring the Right Brain and Left Brain together to act on clues. It allows you to start noticing clues and acting on them, but to do it in a responsible and practical way that will make your Left Brain happy and prevent you from making mistakes while getting closer and closer to your personal treasure. The more you use the Clue Lifecycle, the more you can develop your own "inner compass," your own personal GPS that acts as the wise old mentor on your treasure hunt, pointing out which way to go next.

The Tug of War: What They Don't Teach You at Stanford Business School

Success in the real world is not just about coming up with the right answer, but also about convincing others to go along with that answer, which requires both logic and intuition. Unfortunately, much of our training about business and work leans heavily on the side of logic.

When I attended Stanford Business School, the focus on decision making was almost entirely governed by logic. In fact, we had a whole class about how to create decision models—spreadsheets which had built-in assumptions and showed us the projected cost and benefit of any given "idea" or "new initiative."

We were supposed to base our decisions upon which branch in the spreadsheet, after putting in all the inputs and calculations, was "most optimal" or which provided the best ROI ("return on investment"). The same was true of our negotiation class: we were to lay out, in numbers, the relative benefits and costs of each course of negotiation, and then base our negotiation outcome on these numbers.

Both of these seemed like fantasies to me, even though our grades were based on how well we built our models. Unfortunately, in the real world, things are never so clear as a spreadsheet model, and there is rarely only "one" right answer.

One time I raised my hand in our class and asked our professor, "What if the numbers in the spreadsheet, which are based on assumptions, are wrong?" A little tweaking of the assumptions, I contended, would cause the spreadsheets to give a different answer.

Our modeling professor, Professor Moore, who literally wrote the book (our textbook about modeling using Microsoft Excel, in this case), answered: "The spreadsheets will only get you so far. As for what course of action to take—that's what you, as a manager, are paid the big bucks to do. You can't let the spreadsheets make the decision for you."

In fact, I would contend that logic alone, while helpful in managing an engineering or existing operational process with lots of history, is not very good at making decisions when there is lots of uncertainty in the market or with people. In my own career, working in and being the founder of high-tech start-ups, uncertainty has been a constant companion.

If you are unhappy with your job, or are thinking of

switching careers, or are trying to achieve a level of success or happiness in the business world that you have never seen before, you may be in a period of "high uncertainty" in your life and your career. During a period of "high uncertainty," logic alone isn't enough to help you find your way toward the far, solid shore of success. You need to find your own "inner compass" and "map" to guide you to your destination—even if you have no idea what that destination is.

CASE STUDY NO. 3:
How Logic and Analysis Almost Sank the World's Biggest Company

To show how big this problem is in the business world, let me tell you a story.

In 2005, I met with an old friend who, after attending Harvard for graduate school, had gone back to Detroit and worked in product planning at General Motors.

Some of you will remember that 2005 was toward the end of a phase of "big gas-guzzling cars," from which American automakers made large fortunes. However, as they were flush with cash from the sale of large cars and SUVs, it didn't occur to them to release more fuel-efficient vehicles. Or did it?

At this time, the price of oil (and thus, the price of gasoline) was rising rapidly. Toyota and Honda were starting to make real waves with their hybrid vehicles. Toyota in particular had introduced their *Prius*, which was not only winning awards, but was sold out with a waiting list of many months. Sales of large SUVs were starting to decline, but this was still before the massive economic plunge that would occur soon thereafter in 2008.

I asked my friend why General Motors hadn't come out with a viable hybrid (or electric) car. He said that they had considered it, but that they had done the analysis, and come to the conclusion that hybrids didn't make economic sense for people. They calculated the gas cost savings of hybrid and electric cars, and concluded (very logically I might add!) that people wouldn't buy them.

Since they didn't think people would buy the cars, they didn't put any designs into production in a timely enough manner to stop their decline in sales and profits, which led to some of the largest losses by any corporation in history over the next few years (until General Motors had to be bailed out by the federal government).

Here's an example where someone (perhaps several teams of people) at the biggest car company in the world had the intuition that hybrid and electric cars were the future, but the number crunchers shut down the project. It also shows why we need more intuition in the business world to match up with logic.

What You Will Learn: Navigating with Clues to Find True Success

In this book, through a series of case studies taken from the real world, you'll learn the many ways in which the inner compass of your intuition can speak to you—if you learn to listen and tune in to this language.

As you start to listen to your intuition, you'll find that you need to have a system and criteria by which to judge whether a hunch, dream or coincidence is worth acting on and how fast/slow you should go in pursuing it. This will help you to recognize the clues more clearly by building your own Book of Clues and your own Clue Lifecycle.

Your own Book of Clues is in some ways the most important book you will have, because it will reveal to you, one piece at a time, the Treasure Map of your life and the work you were meant to do in this life. Your Treasure Map isn't just about work, of course; it is about recognizing the people who will make an impact on you in this life and pursuing those relationships.

Just as your clues will be different from mine, your "inner compass" will need to be calibrated differently from mine. If you tend to act too impulsively and only pay attention to the Right Brain, the Clue Lifecycle will help you not only to recognize your clues, but also to act at the right time and after appropriate validation and confirmation. If you tend to be overly cautious and don't follow your intuition when you should, the Clue Lifecycle will help you to recognize clues more quickly, and to act confidently based on your intuition.

Where Do the Clues Come from?

You might wonder, since we are dealing with subjective topics such as dreams and synchronicity, whether the clues really exist and whether there really is a Treasure Map for your life. Or you may have a more "scientific"-minded spouse or sibling who scoffs at the idea that *clues* and Treasure Maps really exist.

One of the main things that I learned at MIT studying

engineering was that all of our scientific knowledge is built on models of reality—they aren't reality itself. If the model seems to produce verifiable results, then the model has some validity. Most models break down somewhere because they cannot represent reality, which is much more complex than we may understand.

In that vein, I encourage you to build your own Book of Clues and your own Clue Lifecycle and verify for yourself how your intuition best talks to you. Clues are subjective, and so my clues and your clues (and the clues of your skeptical friend) will be very different.

We'll explore this question of where the clues come from in some depth, from both a scientific and a spiritual perspective, in Chapter 10, "Where Do Clues Come from? A Spiritual and Religious Perspective," and Chapter 11, "Where Do Clues Come from? A Scientific Perspective." In each chapter, we'll present a different model of how and why clues are there, ranging from traditional angels to New Age guides to quantum physics, which suggests the possibility of both Parallel Universes and Future Selves.

Of course, what matters is how you can follow the clues to connect the dots to find a larger pattern in your life, your own personal, life-spanning Treasure Map. We'll explore this in Chapter 12, "The Tapestry Reveals Itself." Finally, we'll look at how individuals following their own clues can have an impact on the collective lack of consciousness in business in general, in Chapter 13, "Injecting Soul into the Soul-less Machine."

Today, there is a rising awareness in our culture that the most fulfilling jobs and careers have as much to do with knowing ourselves and feeling like we are "on the right track" as they do with résumés, titles, salaries and pay-grades. Recent corporate scandals have only accelerated this awareness. So, the Treasure Map will often be leading you not just in a direction of more money, but of *true success*, your own personal treasure, where you can find more fulfillment and a feeling of integrity and purpose in your life and your work.

"You are standing on the sea-shore and the waves wash up an old hat, an old box, a shoe, a dead fish, and there they lie on the shore. You say: 'chance, nonsense!'

The Chinese mind asks 'What does it mean that these things are together?'"

–Carl Jung
The Symbolic Life

CHAPTER 2

The Book of Clues

Searching for the Holy Grail

In the movie *Indiana Jones and the Last Crusade*, Sean Connery plays the father of the world-famous archaeologist Indiana Jones (played by Harrison Ford). In this installment, we learn where Indiana Jones's fascination with ancient treasures comes from. Indy's father was also a seeker of ancient treasures, and there is one in particular that he's been searching for his entire life: the Holy Grail.

Sean Connery's character recognizes that finding this holiest of artifacts isn't something that's going to happen overnight. In fact, he realizes that the only way to find it is to gather clues about its existence over time, eventually "piecing together" the puzzle over his entire lifetime.

He has a little book, which he has been carrying with him and in which he has recorded clues as they came to him, that he calls his "Grail Diary." Some of the clues are quotes from ancient texts, some are phrases he has heard, some are pictures he's seen and redrawn, and some are just plain intuition and speculation.

Whether or not you believe in the physical Holy Grail, there is something important in this story for those of us looking to bring more integrity, soul and purpose into our lives and work. Our Grail Diary is our own personalized Book of Clues. The clues, taken together, represent our own unique Treasure Map, leading us to our own Holy Grail, our personal definition of *true success*.

My Own Story—Learning to Navigate

By the time I was 35 years old, I had started, grown and sold my stake in several multi-million-dollar high-tech corporations. During this time, my clients had included some of the largest and best-known corporations in the world, including Fidelity Investments, General Motors, *The New York Times*, and Eastman Kodak. Later, when I wanted to do something more creative, I started to work in video games—in the emerging field of social and mobile games, and the games I helped create had millions of players.

Through these start-ups, I have learned to deal with the ins and outs of raising capital, dealing with corporate culture, managing growth and profitability in uncertain times, and different ways of measuring "success."

While many would have considered this a "successful" career on its own, I found that I didn't feel fulfilled or successful when I was measuring my success only by "dollars and cents." Rather, I was the most fulfilled when I had a strong sense of purpose and integrity in my work and life, and I had the feeling of "being in the right place at the right time." In fact, when I was at the "wrong place at the wrong time," the message came in loud and clear that I needed to move on.

I'm not that dissimilar from other successful businessmen and women—except that I openly speak about having used my dreams and intuition as key parts of the decision-making process. I have used them to come up with ideas that entire businesses have been built on, to find ways to leapfrog our competition, to find ways out of difficult business situations, to land new clients, and to "feel" the right direction to follow in my own life—even when the direction wasn't always the most logical one. You will see my own case studies sprinkled throughout this book, along with many men and women I have interviewed over the years about the role their own intuition and clues have played in their lives.

This recognition—that my intuition had been my compass to building a successful career—came slowly at first. Eventually, I recognized the value of the messages that my intuition was sending to me, both during the day and in my dreams.

As I accumulated more and more of these in my own Book of Clues, I started to see my own patterns of clues that I should and shouldn't follow. Over time, this led me to develop my own "navigational system," the Clue Lifecycle, which has served me quite well, not only in being financially successful, but also in feeling more fulfilled in my work, career and life.

Measuring Success: What Is Your Holy Grail?

Finding the Holy Grail in the context of our personal treasure hunt is about figuring out what *true success* means to each of us. More importantly, it means getting in touch with a deeper part of ourselves, the "inner mentor," which knows what our "calling" is in this life. In short, our inner mentor knows the person we were meant to be!

What does being successful mean to you? It could mean a larger salary, a corner executive office, a published book, a successful speaking career, a multi-million dollar house, better health, more responsibility, or it could mean spending time doing more of the things that you love—writing, art, traveling, speaking. Whatever the external parameters of success are to you, the internal parameters are most likely to be that you have more integrity, purpose and meaning in your work.

Similarly, the most successful (and fulfilling) companies have more than good balance sheets and income statements—they also have a sense of *integrity*, *purpose* and *meaning* that today is often lacking in the general business world. The only way for a company to get these qualities is for the founders and managers of the company to align themselves with their own personal sense of integrity, purpose and meaning.

For those of us who live in the business world on a daily basis, I call this lack of integrity, purpose and soul, our "collective dilemma"—because without it at the corporate level, we are confined to being cogs in the soul-less machinery that cranks out profits and losses.

Without it at the personal level, we are constantly left with the feeling that "something is missing" in our careers—a feeling of "un-ful-filled-ness" that can seep into all areas of our lives and lead to our own "personal dilemma."

The good news is that, unlike the Holy Grail in the Indiana Jones movie, which was hidden away and protected by a group of ruthless protectors, our inner mentor *wants* to be found.

This part of us wants us to utilize our gifts, and it wants us to be more successful and passionate in our work and lives. So much so that it's constantly sending us messages—through dreams, through intuition, our "hunches," and even through events in the world around us that seem like coincidences. It is constantly trying to reveal the Treasure Map by sending you clues. We just have to stop interfering with the messages we are getting from this part of ourselves.

Noticing the "Invisible Hand"

Imagine that you are walking into a room full of people who you don't know. Imagine now that you have an invisible "inner mentor" with you, a wise old man (or woman), a veritable Gandalf or Obi-Wan Kenobi, who knows all about where you've been and where you might be going in your path in this life.

Suppose again that this spiritual master has a big pointer and can use it to point out people and things that you should pay attention to in this room.

These might be persons who will be important in achieving your immediate career goals, or someone with whom you'll have a conversation that will lead you in an unexpected direction, or cause you to question something you've been doing that doesn't quite feel right in your life. It could simply be someone you will want to meet and have a romantic relationship with, or maybe even someone who used to live in a place that you might need to visit (or move to) in order to find the next step in your career.

Having this kind of master could be very convenient. The "invisible hand" of this inner mentor could be an incredible help when you have to make decisions about your life, when you are visiting a new place, starting a new project, looking for a new job. And what if this inner master pointed out these clues to you in such a way that you would feel compelled to pay attention to them?

In fact, each of us already has an inner mentor pointing out things that are important for us to pay attention to. It's as if an "invisible hand" was prompting us to notice a particular person, place or thing. We *notice* this thing in such a way that it stands out from its background, and we feel a little *tickle*. This tickle might be described as an "uncanny feeling" and is akin to what some people call *déjà vu*, but it occurs more frequently. It might be thought of as a tug of attention.

CASE STUDY NO. 4:
The "Invisible Hand" Helps Me to Get Unstuck

Let's start with a simple but powerful example in my own life of how the "invisible hand" is at work pointing out clues all the time! These clues don't have to reveal anything as substantial as a new business idea or a script for a blockbuster movie—they can simply help us move to the next step on an endeavor that's important to us but has been lagging of late.

A few years ago, I was having trouble completing a first draft of a manuscript for a book that I had been working on for months. I had come to a certain point and "stalled"; I had written a number of chapters and wanted to write more, but I hadn't felt the creative inspiration that fueled my early writing. I began to worry about if and when I would *ever* finish the manuscript.

I needed something to get me unstuck.

One evening, after work, I was contemplating sitting down at the computer to resume work on the manuscript by writing another chapter. I wasn't feeling particularly "in tune" with the book at the time, so instead of writing, I invented a distraction, which was to clean my room. The room was quite messy and had a lot of my old papers scattered in no particular order.

As I started cleaning out the old papers and artifacts that cluttered the room, my attention was caught by a stack of papers sitting behind some binders. I pulled them out and examined them. I saw that it was an older, early draft of one of my previous books, called *Zen Entrepreneurship*. What drew my attention wasn't the printout or the content of the book, but rather the scribbles all across the manuscript. I had marked my revisions to this early draft in pen and for whatever reason had not thrown away this marked-up copy.

For some reason, I got an "uncanny feeling" when I saw these scribbles, and sat down and started reading some of them. Rather than recognize this first *uncanny feeling* as a clue (which I might have done), I ignored it and went ahead and threw this old manuscript away. After all, it wasn't really useful any more except for sentimental reasons.

As I continued cleaning, I noticed a later draft of the same manuscript, and this one also contained scribbles all over it. I again had the *uncanny feeling* and began to realize that my inner mentor was pointing something out to me.

After I thought about it for a second, it gave me an idea. Rather than sitting down and writing another chapter of my new manuscript, I decided, I should print out a complete manuscript of everything I'd written to date, and start revising and refining it rather than trying to write more. I usually don't do this (do a full printout and start editing the hard copy) until I'm much further along with a manuscript.

Paying attention to the clue, I went ahead and did this, and after months of not making any progress, I found myself not just revising the new manuscript, but naturally "inspired" to write more chapters for the book in the coming days.

The lesson here isn't so much about "writing and revising a manuscript" as about paying attention to clues. I was stuck with my writing; the *uncanny feeling* came when I started cleaning my room, which gave me the clue I needed to know to get "unstuck." After that, the rest of the manuscript rolled out much more quickly and effectively.

The Rules of Treasure Hunting

Throughout this book, I will present to you the *Rules of Treasure Hunting*, which taken together constitute a body of knowledge and guidance about how to find and follow clues. These are "rules of thumb" you can use in different situations. Let's start with the first one:

TREASURE HUNTING RULE NO. 1:

Pay attention to uncanny feelings

The "invisible hand," when at work in our lives, points out elements in our environment—people, places, directions, objects—by "tickling" our unconscious. These clues come from a wiser, deeper part of ourselves than our conscious mind; it often has a good idea of how to solve a particular problem or which direction to follow when we are stuck consciously, because it knows where we are "meant to go," even if we don't recognize it consciously.

Just as I was naturally drawn to my old drafts with my scribbles on them, you might be drawn to something in your own environment—at home, at work, or out at the mall—that contain a "little message" for you. These "little messages" come as part of your intuition, and if you learn to pay attention to uncanny feelings, you can recognize them every single day.

In order to see these clues, you only have to ask yourself: what is my mind naturally drawn to? What in this picture stands out for me? *If you notice something in the outside world, and it feels "unusual," "odd" or "uncanny," then it might be a clue. Write it down.*

You can test this in a library or bookstore. Walk in but don't look for a specific book; instead simply let your mind and eyes wander to see what they are naturally drawn to, and which book titles give you an *uncanny feeling.*

Your Own Personal Book of Clues: the Treasure Map

Of course, clues from your environment are not always as simple and straightforward as this example. Often, you have to monitor *uncanny feelings* which repeat over a period of time to determine what the clues are pointing out to you.

The best way to do this is to have your own Book of Clues.

Just like Sean Connery's character recording clues in his "Grail Diary" about how to find *the* Holy Grail, in order for you to make progress on your own treasure hunt you have to start writing them down and start acting on them. Like Connery's Grail Quest, finding your true calling and contributing to the world through your work are lifelong quests. Your own Book of Clues is just what you need to turn your life and work into a treasure hunt.

Your Book of Clues can be a regular notebook in which you write down your intuitions, hunches, dreams, funny feelings and synchronicities. As you write down more clues, you will start to see patterns, and this becomes a map that will guide you to true success, if you let it. Sometimes you can add links directly in your Book of Clues or add notations to let you know when a clue seems more important.

CASE STUDY NO. 5:

An Everyday Hunch Leads to a New Business

Let's take another example, this one about how a funny feeling led to a whole new business opportunity.

In 2002, Justin, a sales and marketing executive in Boston's once-booming high-tech industry, found himself suddenly without a job. This kind of situation— an unexpected layoff—is often the catalyst for an entrepreneurial adventure. Justin decided that he no longer wanted to work for someone else; that, instead, he wanted to be his own boss and start his own company. The only question was—what company to start?

He found himself sitting on the rooftop deck of his apartment building in Boston's North End when his intuition came calling. He looked at the beach chair he was sitting on, and began to evaluate it with that *uncanny feeling* that would-be entrepreneurs get which constitutes a little "clue." A native of Cape Cod, famous for its beaches, Justin wondered why there weren't any chairs like this manufactured locally.

He found that the chair was built internationally and imported into the U.S. He soon realized that he could create a company that produced hand-made quality beach chairs, bringing together his love for the beach and his interest in sales, marketing and distribution. With that he founded and grew the Cape Cod Chair Company. More importantly, this gave him the opportunity to spend time where he loved to be: on Cape Cod.

I've interviewed entrepreneurs from all around the world and have found that Justin's story, while unique, is not unusual. A series of unexpected, seemingly "random" external events (in this case the layoff and sitting on the rooftop deck), combined with an intuition (in the form of an *uncanny feeling* about the chair), served as the catalyst for a whole new direction in his career. In his case, this conspired with his lifelong interest in spending time on Cape Cod to create a meaningful and purposeful direction in his career—building a business.

Seemingly random external events can be new types of clues that point us in a direction which, if followed, can unlock a larger pattern in our lives. Intuition is the key to unlocking this pattern, and in this book we'll explore different ways to recognize these funny feelings.

The Importance of Repetition

Whenever your inner compass points out something to you, you should note it in your mind, and ideally put it in your Book of Clues later that day.

How do you know when something is a clue and is worth writing down? There is a second Rule of Treasure Hunting:

TREASURE HUNTING RULE NO. 2:

If it repeats, then it's most likely a clue

Like any ability, your ability to recognize relevant clues will improve over time—the important thing is to write down what you think are clues and, if a clue repeats, to take particular note of this clue.

So, basically, if it might be a clue, write it down. Soon you will begin to see patterns in what your attention is being drawn to, and patterns of symbols. This is the process by which we can receive guidance that can help in making decisions.

Time will tell you what it really meant, and by writing clues down now, you will be in a much better position to reflect on them in the future.

All significant clues are marked by the co-relation of an external event with an internal event.

There are many variations of these external events and internal processes. One major type of clue is when a dream (internal event) symbol appears in our waking life the next day (external event). We'll talk in more detail about this specific type of clue in Chapter 6, "Clues that Come in the Night: Everyday Dreams and Synchronicity."

Meanwhile, let's explore the different types of internal and external clues that you should be writing down in your Book of Clues.

External Clues

An "external" clue is something that happens which your mind takes notice of that you might not normally have paid attention to. This could be a conversation that you overhear in a restaurant; it might be something you read that made an impression on you. It could be a sign on a building that you've walked by a dozen times but haven't noticed.

It also refers to things that seem like mere "coincidences." A friend you haven't talked to in years suddenly calls you one night and says something that makes an impression on you. A colleague of yours quits her job very unexpectedly and, for some inexplicable reason, this makes an impression on you and you begin to think more seriously about your own job.

The key to the external clue is to notice *how it makes you feel*. There is an uncanny sensation that happens from an external event that is different from how you normally feel.

Clues don't have to be so obvious—they could be a very small, unusual feeling that is quickly forgotten, but that is then validated later on, as events unfold. Let's take a look at a simple example.

CASE STUDY NO. 6:
Following the Inner Compass Out of Town

Elaine had just moved into a new place in a suburb of Boston called Watertown. It was the first time that she had lived outside of the city, and she was used to working in the city and commuting toward Boston using public transportation. At the time, she was in between jobs and was looking for her next job.

Just after moving in, she saw a bus that was traveling down Arsenal Street away from Boston and out to the next city along that road, Waltham. For some reason, the bus made a "mental impression" on her—she couldn't explain why, as she always commuted the other way, into the city. In fact, she had never even considered getting a job that was out in the suburbs, because she didn't even own a car and relied on public transportation.

This *uncanny feeling* is a perfect example of when our inner mentor points out something that doesn't logically make sense. In fact, it's the fact that *it doesn't make sense logically* that marks it as a tangible clue and not just ordinary deduction.

Within a few weeks, Elaine was contacted about a job out in Waltham, which she interviewed for, and she was given an offer on the spot.

At first, she wasn't sure if the job was right for her—because she didn't have a car and wasn't used to commuting out to the suburbs. When she realized that her daily commute would involve getting on the bus at the exact stop she had noticed it and riding it up Arsenal Street out to Waltham, she realized that the uncanny feeling was her intuition trying to tell her something. It was a clue.

She decided to take the uncanny feeling and the fact that she'd landed the job so easily as important clues, despite her hesitation of working in the suburbs and discomfort about the commute.

In this case, her inner compass "literally" gave her a direction to follow—in this case the direction the bus was following: west. The job ended up being one of her favorite jobs ever, and had a tangible effect on her career and life. It paid better than many of her previous jobs, and she saved up enough money to launch her own website design business.

Synchronicity

A synchronicity, as defined by Jung, is an "a-causal meaningful coincidence." It happens when you have a seemingly coincidental convergence of an inner event, such as a "thought," and an outer event. There seems to be no *apparent* causal relationship between one event (the internal mental event) and the other (the external event).

This could be as simple as you "thinking about a particular topic," and then wandering by a used bookstore and seeing a book on the topic that you were just thinking of, or can be a series of highly unusual events.

A very famous example of synchronicity referenced by Jung was given by the French writer Émile Deschamps. In his writings, Deschamps reports that as he walked into a café in Paris, he noticed a sign saying that they had plum pudding. That gave him a hankering for the dessert, and he recalled the first time he'd had *plum pudding* with a certain Monsieur de Fontgibu, who had brought the recipe for it from England.

In this instance, Deschamps ordered plum pudding, but was told that the café was out of it—the last bit had been taken by an old man sitting in the corner. Lo and behold, to Deschamps' surprise, the man sitting in the corner was none other than Monsieur de Fontgibu himself, the same man who'd offered him plum pudding ten years earlier!

Deschamps' thinking about both "plum pudding" and "Fontgibu" didn't have any clear causal relationship with his finding this café. Nor did it in any way cause the gentleman he had been thinking about to appear unexpectedly at that moment in time, almost ten years after he'd last seen him.

Sometimes a synchronicity repeats itself, revealing a pattern over time. Deschamps went further to describe how a number of years later he attended a party in Paris where they had plum pudding. He remarked to the host that the only thing missing was Monsieur de Fontgibu. There was then a knock on the door, and when they opened it, to their surprise, it was the same Monsieur de Fontgibu, who was in Paris and who had accidentally come to the "wrong" address!

But synchronicities in the business world don't have to be so dramatic—they simply have to involve the confluence of an internal event—a thought, an intuition, a hunch or a dream—with an external event, which, taken together, constitute a "meaningful coincidence."

CASE STUDY NO. 7:
Going on the Road with an RV

Let's look at a much more ordinary example of synchronicity than Jung's story of plum pudding, but one which provided an important clue.

A few years ago, Rebecca starting suggesting to friends and co-workers that she wanted to travel across the country in an RV that summer. In her own words:

> I had no plans made, but had always wanted to do it. I didn't even know if I had the money for it or if my husband could get the time off. Two weeks later, my best friend was at my house with her two-year-old triplets.
>
> She turned to me while changing one of their diapers and said, "I wanted to know if you and the boys wanted to rent an RV this summer and travel cross-country." I immediately smiled. "Did

I tell you that I wanted to travel cross-country in
an RV this summer?" "No," she replied, surprised.

This is a great example of a synchronicity—she had an
internal desire to take an RV, and then suddenly her
friend was suggesting she might want to go on an RV trip,
unsolicited. There is a synchronicity between the external
event and the internal event. Did one cause the other?
It's impossible to say, which is why this was an a-causal
meaningful coincidence. It was a major clue, which
Rebecca acted upon, partly because of the confirmation
provided by her friend. They ended up having what she
later called an "unbelievable trip" that summer.

Internal Clues

Internal clues are very important to familiarize yourself
with. These are feelings that you get before you make
a decision about some course of action. This includes
recognizing the "funny feelings" that come with seeing an
external clue, or noticing some tightening up or tingling
or other sensation in your body at the right time.

One of the most powerful ways to distinguish between a
real message and a superfluous one is to learn to recognize
inner signals, feelings or sensations that alert you that a
message is there. These signals are part of learning to find
the way to "the Holy Grail"—they are like metal detectors
that tell you that a clue is present.

We all have them, but it's only by becoming conscious
of them that we can learn to recognize them. For example,
I usually get a tingling sensation in my forehead area

whenever I encounter something that has a spiritual significance—it's not there when I'm involved in other non-spiritual tasks. Even if I'm excited about something and have a lot of energy, I rarely feel this tingling sensation unless, for me, there is a direct link with one of my life's missions and feeling I'm on the right path.

I have another signal, which is like a gut wrenching that happens when I'm tempted to make a decision that will work out poorly for me. Usually it's because there's a part of me that really wants something done quickly, even though it would be better to wait rather than to rush into it.

I have been able to use this *inner signal* as a clue, telling me I should slow down. Whenever this happens now, rather than making a decision on the spot, or rather than taking the "quick, easy way," I know to slow down and to wait until the next day or maybe even the next week before making the decision. The extra time usually gives me the perspective I need to make the right decision.

Similarly, my idea of an *uncanny feeling* when synchronicity is at work may be completely different from your own idea of an uncanny feeling. We each have to learn to listen to our bodies and spot the internal clues that come with external clues before we can effectively judge how to act on clues.

CASE STUDY NO. 8:

Connecting the Dots from New York to Mexico to China

Michelle Bonn, who lived in upstate New York, was the owner of a small business that helps U.S.-based companies manufacture and source products and materials throughout Asia and Europe, called Expedient Trade.

One day Michelle came across a newsletter and noticed that a colleague of hers was speaking in Chicago, in conjunction with another woman. She followed the link and found out that this "other woman," let's call her Allison, was the owner of a business in Chicago that sourced products from China, and her company had the word "Global" in it.

Michelle couldn't explain why, but when she saw Allison and her company's name her gut felt tight and her heart began to race—as if in a "fight or flight" reaction. Somehow, Michelle knew that she "had to learn more about this woman and her company." This was an *inner signal* prompted simply by seeing Allison's name, and as Michelle researched her background, it seemed they had a lot in common.

Michelle's first clue was the strange reaction of her body when she came across the woman's company name, the second clue was that she was in such a similar business, and yet a third hint was the "sense of certainty" that she would be meeting this woman in the future, though she didn't know how or when.

This was in January. As with most first appearances of a clue, Michelle sat on the idea and didn't act on it right away. Later that year, a friend of Michelle's from Washington DC asked if Michelle could "fill in for her" as a speaker at a conference in Mexico.

This is the kind of "random event" that often indicates that synchronicity is at work in our lives: a cancelled appearance, a chance meeting, a last-minute trip. Michelle agreed and spoke to the audience about "international and fair trade."

The day after her last-minute speaking engagement, a "random" woman approached Michelle at the conference and asked if she could talk with her. She was starting a new venture that involved selling fair trade items to customers in the U.S.A. As they were talking, she mentioned that she was branching out from her current business, which had the word "Global" in it.

Michelle's body had an immediate reaction to the name of the company—again her heart started racing and her stomach grew tight in recognition—this was Allison. "It was an overpowering sensation," says Michelle. Michelle excitedly explained that she had already seen the woman's website (almost nine months earlier) and had been wanting to meet her ever since.

After this initial meeting, Allison introduced Michelle to significant business partners in China and they ended up doing a lot of business together.

This was a perfect example of a synchronicity working itself out over time, from an initial clue, an *inner feeling and knowing* (seeing the name of the company and the website), to an *unexpected coincidence* (the last-minute call to "fill in" for a speaking engagement, which was only peripherally related to Michelle's own business), followed by an actual external event which confirmed the original clue. Upon meeting Allison, an actual event in the world linked up with a desire she had expressed only to herself, and had made no real effort to effect—to meet her.

More about Clues

Here are some important aspects about how clues work that may help you in conjunction with the Rules of Treasure Hunting:

- **Clues often start off in the form of vague feelings.** These are usually feelings about a particular situation, environment or person you have just met. As you learn to recognize these vague feelings and sensations, you can learn to recognize when a clue is surfacing.

- **Clues repeat themselves and get progressively louder.** Writing down the clues that come to you in the form of feelings, dreams and intuition can be instrumental in recognizing the importance of a series of clues over time. In the example I gave with my manuscript, I didn't recognize the message until I saw the second scribbled manuscript. If you ignore clues the first time around, the clues may get louder and louder and repeat themselves in different ways.

- **Sometimes, you'll need to interpret your clues but at other times they'll come in loud and clear.** In many examples, the meaning of a clue is clear. At other times, it may not be so clear, and you'll have to interpret the symbols that are repeatedly occurring. The first step is to notice the clue, the second step is to interpret the clue, and the third step is to act on it. We'll talk more about these steps in Chapter 3, "The Clue Lifecycle: How to Navigate."

- **The timing of clues may vary greatly; some may emerge only one step at a time.** In some cases, a clue may reveal a pattern over a larger timeframe. In other cases, it will be a command that must be acted on right away. That's why it is important to log the clues in your own Book of Clues.

- **The more you act on clues, the more clues you will find.** I have found that clues—whether they are internal or external—must be taken seriously if we are to develop our intuition and expand its impact on our lives. The more that we act on clues, the more clues we will notice.

- **You don't have to seek out clues; they will seek you out, if you are ready to listen.** In many Native American cultures, visions were cultivated by going out into the wilderness and fasting for a period of days. Today, this isn't necessary; you can simply follow the "little messages" that occur to you during the day— following these steps makes having a big "vision" or "dream" much more likely.

- **The more unusual a clue or the feeling associated with an external event is, the more likely it is to be a significant clue.** If you walk by a building (or a co-worker) every day without much ado, then one day get a tingling sensation or just simply notice something about the building (person) that catches your attention, you might be on to a clue.

This brings us to one of the most important aspects of clues, the next Rule of Treasure Hunting:

TREASURE HUNTING RULE NO. 3:

Clues are subjective, so every Book of Clues
is personalized

You and I might walk into the same room and get completely different clues about different topics that are in our minds. The important thing is that the clue will link an external event, person or entity to something that is happening in your own internal mental process. It could be related to a question you've been wondering about ("Which job should I take?"), some action you've been pondering ("taking an RV trip"), a direction you've been searching for ("I'm stuck—how do I get my book moving again?"), or simply an internal memory ("plum pudding") or an internal sensation (goose bumps or tingling or uncanny feelings).

Unlike Indiana Jones who was searching for a single "Holy Grail" and all clues pointed to the same place, we are each searching for our own definition of *true success*, Since the Book of Clues reveals your personal Treasure Map, all of your clues will be subjective. Time to get started with your own.

EXERCISE

Creating Your Own Book of Clues

In learning to bring integrity, soul and purpose into your work and into your life, the Book of Clues can be an invaluable resource. It can be a guidebook, your own personal book of symbols and clues that leads you to your own Holy Grail—that part of you that wants to be found but is often drowned out by the needs of the workplace and our daily lives.

1   Get a notebook to be your first Book of Clues.
    It can be any lined or unlined notebook, though
    I prefer a journal with a meaningful cover image.

2   Throughout the day, take note of when an
    external event invokes an internal feeling that
    is "unusual." This could be a feeling of *déjà vu*,
    an uncanny feeling, goose bumps, or some other
    physical sensation.

3   Write down the clue: record the external event
    and the feeling that it gave you.

4   If you can't do this at work, write the clue down
    afterwards. The process of remembering your
    inner thoughts from the day will actually exercise
    the mental muscles that you should be using.

5   Every time you get a repeat confirmation of a clue or a message, put an asterisk or other symbol beside it to let you know that this clue may be significant and is repeating itself.

What if you write down a clue that doesn't point anywhere? That's totally fine—as it's all part of the process of learning to build your own inner compass, your personal GPS that will reveal the Treasure Map of your life and work to you, over a period of time.

The process of writing down possible clues—i.e. when you think that your intuition might be pointing out something to you—will be like starting to flex a muscle that most of us under-use. The more you flex this muscle, the more messages and clues you'll recognize in your own life.

CHAPTER 3

The Clue Lifecycle:
How to Navigate

Learning to Navigate

The Phoenicians were famous for navigating their boats based on the position of the stars. Over time, they were able to use their knowledge to develop a navigational system that was so precise they could find very specific islands in the middle of the ocean from a thousand miles away. These insights about using the stars for navigation were accompanied by one of the first written alphabets; probably one of the reasons for the development of their writing was to keep track of how to navigate from one point to another—a "body of knowledge" they would have prized above all others.

This chapter is about learning to use your own clues as a way to navigate a different set of very treacherous waters: the vast oceans of the business world in *general*, and the more personal waterways of your career and personal life *in particular*.

By learning to follow the rhythm of your own clues, by learning to pay attention to synchronicity and the odd inner sensations that accompany it, you can get a better understanding of how the "invisible hand" works for you.

If you think of your own particular Book of Clues as your very own Treasure Map, then, as you collect and act on clues, you will develop your very own body of knowledge about how to navigate using clues: which clues are important, what direction a clue is likely leading you in, and when to take action or to sit on a clue and wait for the next one.

In my own case, it took many years of seeing clues and getting "confirmation" before I really started to trust the "invisible hand" of my inner mentor as it pointed out external clues to me. It took even longer to figure out which clues to follow and which ones I needed to wait for more confirmation on before taking action. This was the birth of the Clue Lifecycle, which we'll explore in this chapter. Now, the emergence of the "invisible hand" and the feelings associated with it are a welcome sign that something interesting may be about to happen. I have learned to anticipate it with a spirit of playfulness.

Where Are the Clues Leading You? One Clue at a Time

The process of finding and following clues reminds me a little of the hit TV series *Columbo*; each episode would start out with a mystery, and as the episode progressed a series of clues would emerge—leading the detective to uncover a pattern of events that was always there—but invisible to him in the beginning. Sometimes one clue led clearly to the next clue; sometimes the clues came out of order and didn't make sense *until* the next clue had been uncovered.

To bring more integrity, soul and purpose to the world of business and into your own career, you should learn to be like Columbo—looking to solve the mystery that is the larger pattern of your life and your work. You may only have inklings of this larger pattern, or you may know certain parts of it consciously. As you follow the clues, you may find this larger pattern being revealed to you, like a puzzle in which the pieces are filled in one at a time, to reveal a beautiful, coherent image.

The larger pattern of your Treasure Map may have a mystical or spiritual component. But that doesn't mean you have to spend all of your time on "mystical" or "spiritual" pursuits to go treasure hunting. Quite the opposite. I would encourage you to use the clues and messages that are already coming to you, on a daily basis, to get *practical* results in the real world.

More specifically, this chapter is about how clues are really pointing you in possible directions that *you may decide to pursue*. It is always up to you whether you want to follow through with one and to what extent.

This is where the integrated view of the Right Brain and the Left Brain are necessary not just to make a decision about a direction, but also to convince others to go along with you.

In the business world, it's often difficult to justify that you are taking an action because "you saw it in a dream" or it came through "serendipity" (more on how to talk about these things in the business context in Chapter 7, "Bringing the Clues into the Board Room").

Synchronicity: the Key to Unlocking a Clue

Thus far, we have talked about the first stage of getting a clue, the *intuition* stage—when you first notice the clue and the odd feelings that come with it. This might include clues that come to you in the form of Big Dreams, or everyday messages—the hunches, funny feelings that come when your inner mentor is pointing out something or someone that you need to pay attention to.

But the recognition of a possible clue isn't enough for

it to qualify, by itself, as something that should be acted on immediately. Recognizing a clue is simply a way for you to notice that there is something "in play" here, and you should pay attention and be open to what happens next. We cannot always predict where a particular clue will lead us—this usually takes the emergence of a series of clues over time.

While each of these kinds of clues can be a navigational aid in and of themselves, the key to recognizing them is often to learn to pay attention to synchronicity. Remember that a *synchronicity* is a "meaningful coincidence," the coming together of an "inner event" (such as a hunch, thought, daydream, sleeping dream or intuition) and an "outer event" which relates to the inner event, but with no *apparent* causal relationship between the events.

When you notice a synchronicity, that is your cue that a particular clue is important at this point in your life. Since the "clues" are meant to reveal an underlying pattern in your life that you may not be aware of consciously, it can take a while for this pattern to emerge.

So, back to the question that we asked earlier: how do you know when something is a real "clue" and not just happenstance? Always remember the first two Rules of Treasure Hunting: (1) if it's unusual or produces an "uncanny" sensation, and (2) if it repeats, then it's probably a clue.

CASE STUDY NO. 9:
All Clues Point to Florida

Let's start with a very simple example. The most common

example of synchronicity is one that we have all had—you find yourself thinking about someone who you haven't seen in a while. Suddenly, within a few days, this person calls (or emails, or visits you), out of the blue.

This is the confluence of an inner event (your thinking about this person) and an outer event—the call, email or appearance. There is no visible causal relationship (Jung would call it an *a-causal* relationship) between the inner and the outer event—the person calls or emails out of the blue, sometimes many months or years since you've last heard from them.

Can this simplest type of "clue" help you become more successful in business or to discover your work in this life?

It depends on what happens next, and where that phone call or email leads you. Let's take an example of my own: This happened when I started my very first start-up, Brainstorm Technologies, which I started in my living room back in 1993. I didn't know very much about starting a software company, but was excited to do so.

The first part of the clue involved my friend Mario, and the second part involved Florida. Notice how the clues repeat and overlap with each other—like disparate threads coming together to weave a tapestry that I was not consciously aware of at first.

Mario had been a co-worker at Lotus Development Corporation (one of the largest software companies in the world at the time) when I first started thinking seriously about starting a company—in fact, Mario and I had brainstormed doing a start-up together many times.

One day, he abruptly departed Lotus, and decided to go

and spend time quite literally "on the beach" in Florida. The circumstances of his departure had left me with an *uncanny feeling* that he might have something to do with starting a company in the near future. This is the kind of clue that I have subsequently learned to pay attention to, but at the time, I didn't think too much of it.

Six months or so passed, and I went ahead and started the company with my roommate and fellow MIT alum, Mitch. We were working in the living room of our little bachelor pad, when I suddenly had a dream with Mario in it. I began to wonder what he was up to. Suddenly, the next day, seemingly out of the blue, I received a phone call from Mario. As I hadn't heard from him in six months, this time I realized something unusual had happened and I paid attention to this clue.

Mario had been living "on the beach" in Florida, but was just back in Boston and needed a place to crash for a few days. I took the fact that he had appeared out of nowhere just as we were getting close to launching our first product as a good sign. He was very interested in what we were doing and we toyed with the idea of having him join us as a third co-founder. In fact, if you'd asked me the significance of this clue at the time, I would've said that it meant Mario was going to join us.

But clues are a little more complicated than that in the real world. In the end, that particular angle didn't work out. In deciding that he wasn't going to work with us but was going to head back to Florida, Mario then gave us the idea that we should go to a conference to be held in Florida within the next month. This was the big technology conference for Lotus-related technologies that was in its inaugural year. I had vaguely heard of the conference before but we hadn't been planning to go.

In fact, we were very short on cash in those days as we were busy building our first product. But Mario kept insisting that we should go, since it would be the perfect place to showcase our product. At Mario's behest, we eventually realized that the conference was probably a good idea. Partly on his advice, we decided to borrow the money from Mitch's parents that would be needed to get a booth to exhibit at the conference in Florida.

It turned out to be one of the best decisions of the early days of our new company. The booth gave us significant visibility and we were swamped with people who wanted to buy our product. For many years, we would consider our trip to Florida the place where we "launched" the company. We got more than enough customers at that conference to take care of all of our expenses and more.

The Threads Weaving Together

This example shows the complex workings of synchronicity: a series of clues, each suggesting a thread that weaves itself into an interesting pattern over a period of time. The threads of synchronicity, revealed to us in specific clues, when acted upon, weave together into a tapestry that is part of our life-spanning Treasure Map.

At the time, I was just following my intuition, unaware of what particular pattern might be emerging. Here are some of the clues and the threads that played out:

- Mario leaving *Lotus* when I was still thinking of starting a company left me with the *uncanny feeling* that his departure was important.
- Mario going to *Florida* to hang out "on the beach."
- The subsequent starting of our company around *Lotus* technology.
- My dream of Mario at that time, and his appearance a few days later, from *Florida*.
- One possible direction from the clue was having Mario join us in starting the company. This didn't work out; he decided to go back to *Florida*.
- Another possible direction from the clue, which Mario suggested, even insisted on, was that we should go to the *conference* in *Florida sponsored by Lotus*.
- Our subsequent attendance at the *conference*, and very successful *launch* of our product in *Florida*.

Of course, each company and career path is different. The point here is not that you should think about going to a conference in Florida, but that even a synchronicity as simple as *thinking of a friend and having them call you out of the blue* can be an important development. It can be a "clue" that uncovers threads that have a significant impact on your life and career.

The Full Clue Lifecycle

This sequence of events demonstrates almost all of the stages of what I have come to call the Clue Lifecycle. The Clue Lifecycle is a series of stages, starting with the recognition that you have a clue on your hands, through the process of confirming the clue, acting on it, validating and reflecting on the experience, and going on to the next clue. The stages are shown in Figure 1 and explained below.

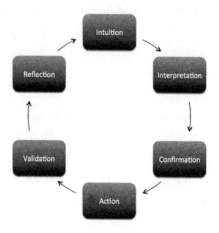

Figure 1: The Clue Lifecycle.

This brings us to the next Rule of Treasure Hunting:

TREASURE HUNTING RULE NO. 4:

Apply the stages of the Clue Lifecycle to your clues, playfully and repeatedly

---

Let's go through the stages of the Clue Lifecycle individually.

- **Intuition.** The stage when a clue first emerges is the *intuition* stage. This could be any type of clue that we've been discussing—the important thing is that the clue leaves you with an odd sensation, and that you (hopefully) write it down in your Book of Clues.

The *intuition* is usually a signal to *pay attention* to something that your inner mentor is pointing out to you, alerting you to its presence by an internal feeling or sensation.

- **Confirmation.** A *confirmation* usually comes from a synchronistic event that results in a repetition of the clue, or of some element from an initial clue. In the example I just gave, it was 1) thinking about my friend Mario and 2) having him call me out of the blue. The *confirmation* could be confirmation that this is a real clue, or it could be confirmation of the "timing" or "direction" that the clue is indicating. It may not be obvious *what* pattern the clues fall into right away, but the confirmation of the clue is a signal that *something is definitely up, this is not some random occurrence. Get ready.*

- **Interpretation.** It's the next stage, *interpretation*, that is the most interesting and perhaps most difficult. The clue is telling you something, but what is it? Usually it is a path that you may want to try out that may be different from the one you thought you were on. The *interpretation* of the clue is critical but don't be too hard or fixed on your initial interpretation. In the example that I just gave, I thought the interpretation was that Mario was going to join us as a third co-founder. We gave this a try, but it didn't work out—which often happens. Not every thread is meant to be followed right away. However, he did lead us down a very important path—the conference in Florida—that we would *otherwise* not have followed. Like some dreams, clues can be thought of as symbols that need to be interpreted, and this stage is about identifying a possible direction that you might want to "try out."

Before we continue, it's important to note that though the stages are listed in order, they don't necessarily pan out that way in real life. Sometimes you will get confirmation that a clue is important by seeing it more than once before you have any idea what it means. At other times, you might interpret a clue right away, and then you get confirmation via repetition.

- **Action.** After intuition, interpretation and confirmation, you should think about taking *action* based on the clue. With most clues, this is only a matter of "trying out" something, so this is easy to do. This is where you have to be careful—your clue might be that you need a new job, but it doesn't mean that you should quit your job right away. It means you should take a step in that direction and see what opens up for you.

  There are two types of actions—one is a simple "honoring" of the clue by taking some concrete little action—we will explore this idea in subsequent chapters. The other is actually moving in the direction a clue is suggesting in your life. A small action, from a dream or a clue, can be as simple as going to meet someone for a cup of coffee, watching a movie that the clue reminds you of or drawing a picture—it doesn't have to be a big commitment.

You of course have to use your *discrimination* at this stage; if something seems dangerous or reckless, I wouldn't act on the clue right away. For example, if you're married and you're thinking of an old girlfriend or boyfriend, and they suddenly appear out of the blue and suggest going away for a weekend—well, this is definitely an interesting clue, but it may not be a good action to take, for obvious reasons!

In my example, we first tried working with my friend Mario as another co-founder, honoring the clue even though that path didn't work out. I was still open to where it might lead: though we didn't have enough money for the conference in Florida, we nonetheless decided to go. Using our discrimination, it seemed like a very reasonable step to take for a small software company—and so we borrowed the money to go to the conference. It was a good decision from both an intuitive and a logical place. The action step should take into account both the Left Brain and the Right Brain.

- **Validation and Reflection.** These are really two stages that are related. The first part is about validation. Did the action make sense? Did it move us in the right direction? Reflection has a double meaning here—to *reflect* on the action that you may or may not have taken (was it validated?), and the *reflection* of the original clue in the environment around you, usually with the appearance of additional confirmation.

In our case, reflecting on the first possible path of action didn't work out, but the second path turned out to be one of the most important business decisions we made in those days. We first validated the action from both an intuitive and logical perspective, making sure it made sense to borrow money to go—we decided it did if we could get the product done by the conference so it would be a "launch" event. The validation after we acted was easy—the conference was a big success, and we sold enough of our product to pay back the money we borrowed and to launch the company in earnest.

The reflection stage happens after the action has been validated or invalidated. It may happen in strange and mysterious ways that result in an additional confirmation of the original clue or a new one.

At the conference in Orlando, we had been so successful that we decided to skip the closing ceremony of the conference and instead drove to the Florida coast.

There we unwound for a few hours before starting our trip back to Boston. It was a beautiful day, though partly cloudy on the beach near Tampa, and there were very few people around—the seagulls were everywhere. I held up a French fry and the seagulls flocked to it, flying in from all over the beach and swarming around me. It was a little scary, but I had to laugh because this seemed to be a very apt *reflection* of what had happened at the conference: we had held out our product and been swamped by people wanting to buy it. And hanging out on the "beach" after a conference about Lotus reminded me of the odd sensation I'd had many months earlier when my friend Mario left Lotus to go and "hang out on the beach."

While this sounds like a linear process, it doesn't need to be. The Clue Lifecycle isn't meant to be a "rigid" structure that must be followed slavishly, but rather is a way of thinking about intuition that comes to us in the form of clues. Because the more a clue overlaps, the more unusual it is, the more significant it might be at some point in the future—this structure can help guide us.

A significant series of synchronistic events doesn't necessarily have only one beginning and one ending—it can be an on-going cycle of synchronicities, each of which might have their own Clue Lifecycles, and each of which eventually reveals threads that weave a larger pattern. Sometimes, years after the original event, a synchronicity might show itself again. If it does, then you know that the pattern is still evolving.

The Hard Thing about Clues

The best way to learn to recognize these experiences is to practice by paying attention to clues that are happening all around you. When clues repeat, that's when you know that "something is up"!

By far the most difficult part of these tasks is not recognizing the clue—but recognizing the path of action the clues may be leading you to try out—a *possible* path or future that is being laid out in front of you.

Sometimes, the clue needs to be interpreted; at other

times, the clue and the directions being implied are quite obvious. In the preceding example, we thought it pointed in one direction—but it ended up pointing in another. As it turned out, Mario suggested we go to the conference in Florida, which meant there was no *interpretation required.*

Quite often, though, there is some interpretation required. And sometimes a single clue has many levels of intertwined meanings. In psychological speak, we would say that the "clue" contains symbols that are *over-determined.* Freud used this term to refer to dream symbols, which often had many different meanings. Here's a simple example to chew on.

CASE STUDY NO. 10:
Living between the Worlds

In the fall of 1997, four years after the initial launch of our product, I left Brainstorm, the start-up that I had co-founded and had been running for four years.

While I wasn't sure what I wanted to do next, I kept seeing images and statues of mermaids in various places in New England—statues at restaurants, pictures on walls, in gift shops, etc. This was made more unusual by the fact that I had been to these places before; I just hadn't noticed that there were mermaids on the walls and everywhere I looked.

This is a perfect example of how the "invisible hand" of the inner mentor works—it points out things in the environment that may have been in plain sight before but hadn't been *noticed* by our conscious minds. The inner mentor then produces the feelings of unusual-ness so that you recognize you are being given a clue!

I had no idea what this mermaid imagery meant, but I kept seeing it—in shop windows, in books, and on and on. Whenever I noticed one, I would have that "funny feeling"—the "odd sensation" that something was in play beyond my normal sight.

This was a symbol, I realized, and, as with symbols that come in dreams, I understood that it might need interpretation before I could recognize where the clue was leading me. As I thought about possible interpretations, I came to the realization that a mermaid to me represented someone who lived in between two worlds—the fish world of the ocean and the human world of land. Many a good movie (*Splash, The Little Mermaid*) has been made about the challenges and difficulties that mermaids face by being "in between" worlds.

At the same time as I began noticing the mermaids, I had started thinking seriously about going to California to live in Silicon Valley. But I still liked the idea of living in Boston, and didn't want to sell my condo. I was ruminating on some workable solution to the problem and wanted to become "bi-coastal" for a time—I could try out the west coast while still keeping one foot on the east coast.

Many of my friends, however, doubted that I could live in both worlds—the east and west coast—or cope with the difficulties of doing so, particularly going back and forth every few weeks, not to mention the cost and need for a stable income.

I took the mermaid clue as a confirmation that it was

possible to live in both worlds, and I went ahead and spent the first six months of 1998 living on both coasts, traveling back and forth every few weeks.

It turned out to be one of the best decisions that I have ever made, not only because I had such a great time in California. More importantly, it gave me time and space to begin writing, which led to a second career, becoming an author. The mermaid theme of living in two worlds was reflected in my thoughts concerning my career: to be a computer software entrepreneur and a writer—two very different parts of the business world, but it is possible to thrive in both.

What I started writing about was another "reflection" of the "mermaid" theme—of living in two worlds—about living in the business world, and living in the world of spiritual experiences: dreams, synchronicities, creative flashes and spiritual wanderings. The book I started writing was called *Zen Entrepreneurship*.

This is an example of over-determinedness, or multiple levels of meaning packed into a single one: the *clue* pointed out something that was an issue for me in my life at that time (east coast vs. west coast), as well as an overarching theme in my life (co-existence in two worlds—business and spiritual), and pointed toward a solution as being right for me at the time.

In fact, "living between the worlds" is an apt description for someone who pays attention to the wisdom that comes to us in our dreams and through synchronicity, and who also lives in the sometimes harsh but rewarding world of business.

To Act or Not to Act—Bring the Right Brain and Left Brain Together

The fundamental question remains: how do you know when to act on a clue and when not to? Therein lies one of the paradoxes of synchronicity—the more you "trust yourself" to follow your intuition, the more often you will get intuition that's helpful and meaningful.

But how do you get the confirmation that will let you trust your intuition more? It sounds like a chicken-and-egg question. I assure you, however, that if you start writing down your clues, and even take tentative actions to try out the directions suggested by them, you'll start to navigate with more confidence.

You don't always have to take literal action based on the dream or clue right away; you can reflect on the more general direction or theme that's being expressed by the clues and symbols and take small steps to move in that direction, before you look for more validation.

Knowing when to act and when not to also depends on reflecting on your own personal patterns. Are you someone who jumps into things quickly without doing your homework? Does this occasionally get you into trouble? Or are you someone who doesn't jump in and misses opportunities when you should have done so?

The transition between *confirmation, interpretation* and *action* can be managed by paying attention to your habitual patterns and compensating for them. If you are someone who uses too much of the Left Brain, looking for analytical answers (as in the example I gave about my friend at General Motors), then the way to use the Clue Lifecycle is to jump in and do some "half-step" or action that you can use to validate the direction for yourself.

If you are the opposite, and rely only on the Right Brain, the intuitive creative side, and don't tend to think things through, then you should pause after you see/recognize a clue. If it's important, it will repeat, and then you can act after you have received the clue several times. We will explore this idea of building your own personal patterns into your Clue Lifecycle in more detail in Chapter No. 8 "Anti-Clues: Patterns and Dragons."

For the moment, this brings us to our next Rule of Treasure Hunting:

TREASURE HUNTING RULE NO. 5:

Clues usually indicate timing or direction,
but rarely both

Over many years of noticing and following clues, I have noticed that clues often indicate direction, but not necessarily timing. Or sometimes they indicate timing but not necessarily direction. Rarely do they do both.

This can be frustrating as we try to navigate during our treasure hunt. If you learn to stay with the clues and follow the Clue Lifecycle, not only can this reduce frustration, but it can also help you to see the pattern as more clues emerge over time.

Oftentimes, you might have a clue go through the entire cycle and think that it has served its purpose. Any important clue will live on well past its initial appearance, perhaps even months or years later. Clues often reveal threads in our lives that form underlying patterns that we may or may not be aware of consciously. These threads often intersect and are woven into very complex patterns that result in our particular life path. That's why it's important to write down your clues in your Book of Clues and to mark those which may be pointing you toward something in the future, but which you aren't quite ready for yet.

In Chapter 12, "The Tapestry Reveals Itself," we talk more about looking at "series of clues" over a larger period of time.

Learning to Navigate in Your Own Way

While it may not be immediately apparent what a clue is telling you, if you learn to trust yourself and "go with the clues," you're bound to get very good ideas on the messages and to intuitively feel out the possible paths that you are being "led" on by the "invisible hand."

Even if you don't know exactly where a clue is leading you, and don't take any action right away, by noticing and reflecting on the clues you are receiving, you've started on your own unique path to trusting your inner guidance as you build up your Book of Clues.

By learning to navigate in your personal and professional life using your own personalized clues, you are devising your own personalized navigational system. This system, like that of the Phoenicians long ago, will allow you to hone in on areas of importance and fulfillment in your life.

Using the Clue Lifecycle—*intuition, interpretation, confirmation, action, validation and reflection*—is an on-going process. Once you start it, the process goes on indefinitely, because you are always being led to the right place at the right time in your life. Like episodes of a TV show that reveal a season-long plot over time, your individual Clue Lifecycles will reveal the larger pattern of your Treasure Map to you over time.

You may find yourself following the cycle, stopping the cycle, and letting it go, only to find yourself picking up this thread a year or more later, spurred by a new clue which reminds you of the old one. This intertwining of cycles is very representative of how patterns emerge when we are learning to follow our inner guidance in the real world.

The important thing is to learn to take the first few steps of following that *uncanny feeling* down unexpected paths using your intuition, your dreams and synchronicity to guide you.

This could be simply walking into a second-hand bookstore and randomly finding a book on a subject you were just thinking about, or taking a moment on your way to work and driving down a road that you've been passing by day after day but have never explored. Or it may start by calling someone you haven't talked to in a while but whose image just popped up in your mind.

Taking the first step like this can lead to interesting adventures that you may not have anticipated ... and that is what makes it so much fun.

EXERCISE

Learn to Use the Clue Lifecycle

The goal of this exercise is to learn about the Clue Lifecycle. Remember, this doesn't mean you have to follow the steps slavishly; rather, you must try to understand which stage of the Clue Lifecycle each of your clues is in.

By now, you should already be writing down clues when they come to you. Take a recent clue and figure out which stage you think the clue is at in the Clue Lifecycle.

1   **Intuition.** By default, the clues are all in the first stage when you notice them. The feelings that are associated with the clue are the important tip-off.

2   **Interpretation.** If you have had some repetition/ confirmation, ask yourself, what possible direction might this clue be telling me to go in? It's OK if you don't get this right; the idea is to try to figure out what it might mean. Write down briefly what you think the clue is telling you.

3   **Confirmation.** Repetition is the confirmation that a clue is important. Does this clue relate to an earlier clue in any way? If so, you are at the confirmation stage, because of repetition.

4   **Action.** Ask yourself if you can take a step in this direction to validate the course of action. If you can, try to do it. Start with something small—it might

mean emailing someone or calling them, or visiting some place you haven't been to in a while.

5 **Validation.** Did the action seem to be the right one? What happened? If it was the right one, it might be opening up another clue or further direction for you. If it wasn't the right one, then you can go back to stages No. 2, No. 3, and No. 4—wait for another confirmation, reinterpret the clue and then take some small action. The reason for taking a small action is to see if the universe meets you halfway. If it does, then you have some validation and might be ready to go all the way.

6 **Reflection.** Reflect on the series of the clues that got you where you are. Is there something in the environment confirming what you just did? If so, where is the next clue in this series? If this clue was related to a previous clue, make a link back to it.

As you reflect on the clue, try to see how the dots connect, if at all. What is the larger pattern, your own personal Treasure Map that these clues are revealing to you?

" Sometimes a dream almost whispers ... it never shouts. Very hard to hear.

So you have to, every day of your lives, be ready to hear what whispers in your ear."

—Steven Spielberg

PART II

THE HUNT

CHAPTER 4

Catching Clues while Awake: Synchronicity and Funny Feelings

The best way to get inspired to view your life and career as a treasure hunt is to read and hear examples of others who have followed their clues. After that, of course, the best way to get comfortable intuiting, confirming, interpreting and taking action on clues is to *practice* doing so in your own life.

As you begin to notice individual clues, and write them down in your Book of Clues, you may start to see a set of patterns. As you learn to follow the Clue Lifecycle, you will find that some clues repeat and some don't, but that doesn't mean you shouldn't write them down or pay attention to them.

In this chapter, we are going to focus on clues that occur during the day, at work or outside of work. In the next few chapters, we're going to pay particular attention to clues that come in the night—in the form of dreams.

The Questions to Ask while Treasure Hunting

As you go through the examples of the "invisible hand" at work in the following stories, let's keep the Rules of Treasure Hunting we have encountered thus far in mind. Each of these rules has a corresponding question you can ask.

- **Treasure Hunting Rule No. 1: If you notice something in the outside world, and it feels unusual or uncanny then it might be a clue.** The feeling that is associated with an external or internal event is very important, because it reflects that this "clue" was meant for you. This could be a feeling of *déjà vu*, goose bumps, a feeling of excitement or rush of energy, or just a funny, indescribable feeling. *Question: Is it unusual?*

- **Treasure Hunting Rule No. 2: If it repeats itself, then it's most likely a clue.** Repetition is usually the cue that you have stumbled on a clue. Synchronicity relies on repetition—an inner thought and an outer event. *Question: Does it repeat?*

- **Treasure Hunting Rule No. 3: Clues are subjective, so every Book of Clues is personalized.** If you and I walk into the same room, we are likely to get a different set of clues. Since each of us has our own personal Treasure Map we are trying to uncover, it's important that a clue means something to you and is not just a "generic" clue. For example, you might see a *Star Wars* reference. It's not enough. What does *Star Wars* mean to you? Who did you originally see the movie with? Who is your favorite character in *Star Wars? Question: Does it mean something to you?*

- **Treasure Hunting Rule No. 4: Apply the stages of the Clue Lifecycle to your clues, playfully and repeatedly.** A good understanding of the stages of the Clue Lifecycle will help you to understand how clues evolve over time. Some will be clues you are getting for the first time (intuition), some will have some repetition (confirmation), some you may be moving forward on (action), and some you may be validating action you've already taken, and some may have gone all the way around the Lifecycle and you are reflecting on it by looking for the next clue. *Question: What Stage of the Clue Lifecycle is your clue in?*

- **Treasure Hunting Rule No. 5: Clues usually indicate direction, or timing, but rarely both.** One of the most frustrating things about being on a treasure hunt that spans your whole life is that clues might point out the correct direction, but the timing may be off. For example, you might get an unmistakable clue that writing a particular book is part of your life path, but writing a book can be a multi-year experience, and publishing it can take even longer. *Question: What direction is the clue pointing you in?*

Once you learn to recognize clues, you will find that they are coming to you every day, which is why it's a good idea to write them down. At any given time, you may have multiple clues that are at different stages of the Clue Lifecycle.

As you learn to recognize clues and follow the Clue Lifecycle, you will find that it's not so much a "thing" that you do now and then, but rather has become a continual process that happens as you travel through your day.

CASE STUDY NO. 11:

An Unexpected UFO-related Repetition on the Same Day

Repetition is the key to recognizing a clue, but you may not know exactly where the clue is leading. Here's something that happened to me recently that involved synchronicity and repetition.

I was at a conference in Phoenix about UFOs. Some of you may know that I was an executive producer on two of the most successful UFO documentaries of all time: *Thrive: What on Earth Will It Take?* by Foster and Kimberly Gamble, and *Sirius*, about the life and work of Dr. Stephen Greer.

While at this conference in Phoenix, I walked by a gentleman who I recognized—his name was Danny and I had met him at the Gambles' house after we had made *Thrive*. I said "hello" to him and he immediately asked me about another person who had been in the film, a prominent alternative physicist named Nassim. He had heard a story about him and wondered if I knew anything about it. I had actually never met Nassim in person, even though he had been featured prominently in our film. Danny was on his way to be interviewed so he didn't have much time to talk—he stopped just long enough to ask me that one question. I was left with a funny feeling that this wasn't a random question.

Q: Is it unusual? Yes. Since I hadn't spoken with Danny in over a year, and he had never asked me about Nassim before, I took this as a "possible" clue. Moreover, the funny feeling I had about it made it even more likely that there was a clue in this chance encounter.

Later that same day, I missed my flight to Los Angeles (where I was going for another conference), and ended up taking a later flight. This was unusual for me—I almost never miss a flight. It left me with another funny feeling, since this was a couple of unusual events in a row. As I said earlier, when you miss a flight or some coincidence changes your plans, you should be aware that, as Sherlock Holmes would say, the *"game is afoot,"* and you are likely to see more clues on the way.

I arrived at the Hilton hotel in Los Angeles after a long day, and was dismayed to see a long line at the check-in. I recalled that I had signed up for the Hilton Honors program some time ago, even though I didn't have my number with me; I thought I'd give it a shot and ended up behind a man with long hair and a slight beard who looked vaguely familiar.

In fact, he looked like Nassim, the physicist that Danny had asked me about earlier that day.

When I got to the counter, he and an associate were standing there talking to the front-desk attendant for a long time, right next to me, and I struck up a conversation. It was in fact the same Nassim. The funny thing is that he was speaking at that conference, a fact which I had been completely unaware of.

Q: Did it repeat? Yes, in fact this is what made it unusual: the fact that his name came up and then I chanced to meet him, both on the same day.

Here was someone I had been loosely associated with through a film made almost four years earlier, but whom I had never met, yet in one day his name not only came up unexpectedly but, after missing my original flight, I ended up standing next to him!

Q: Was it personalized? Yes, it was very specific to me, since the clue centered around two people in a film that I had been an executive producer of: *Thrive.*

Q: In what direction was the clue pointing? I wasn't sure, but I started speaking to Nassim and set up a time to meet him as a follow-on action to this clue. Note that in this case, as in many other cases, I didn't have time to write down the elements of the clue—it all happened on the same very busy day. When I met him later at the conference, Nassim then invited me to visit his lab, which I didn't have time to do in the near term. As I write the final draft of this manuscript, six months after this clue, I am going to visit another friend who works with Nassim and I find myself once again invited to visit his lab, which I have only just now scheduled.

Where Does One Clue Lead?

Where does this clue lead? To be honest, I'm not sure yet, and this brings us to the next Rule of Treasure Hunting.

TREASURE HUNTING RULE NO. 6:

In every good hunt, one clue leads to the next

If you act on a clue, it will lead you . . . to the next clue. If I hadn't struck up a conversation and set up a time to meet with Nassim at the conference, that might have been the end of that sequence of clues.

In some of the stories in this book, it will be obvious why a particular clue happened. In others, the clues will simply be indicating a direction. It's very possible that you won't know exactly where the clue is leading you, except to nudge you in a direction and challenge you to pay attention to it.

This was the case with the physicist. I acted on the initial set of clues and met with him. Now I need to act on the next step, and visit him in his lab, which I am about to do as I write this book.

In a further clue, it turned out that one of the people I was at the conference in LA to meet was working just down the road from Nassim's lab. It seems a good bet, then, that these clues were indicating direction, which if and when I am able to follow it, will reveal the next clue.

You may not know *a priori* where the next clue will lead you, but like Indiana Jones, if you follow the clue, it will get you closer to the eventual treasure.

CASE STUDY NO. 12:
The Errant Phrase: Not All Those Who Wander Are Lost

Another type of clue that you should pay attention to is a phrase that you overhear which leaves you with a funny feeling. It means that your inner compass is steering you toward something. The key lies in the intensity of the feeling evoked, or if that isn't enough, as with most clues, if it repeats, it's most probably a clue.

Let's examine a story about Lisa, who was thinking of buying property in Arizona a few years ago. This was during the "housing bubble" before the crash of 2008. She was getting frustrated because she had looked at dozens of places and none of them felt right, but it seemed like everyone else she knew was buying the right house easily.

She ran across the phrase "Not all those who wander are lost" while surfing the web. She wasn't familiar with the phrase and ignored it. Then she saw it again, quoted in a book. This time she had the funny feeling that it might be important.

Q: Was it unusual? It left her with an unusual feeling, but she decided she had no idea what it was about. This is often the case with clues when they initially appear. The intuition stage is about recognizing the clue. The confirmation stage involves waiting for it to repeat.

Then, as sometimes happens in these cases, the universe made it abundantly clear that she was to pay attention to this phrase. She had a long drive home from an event, and there was a car in front of her, which had a bumper sticker on it: "Not all those who wander are lost"!

This was the third time she had seen the phrase, and to hammer it in, the car with the bumper sticker was in front of her for the better part of an hour, so there was no chance she'd miss the clue!

Q: Did it repeat? Yes, it had happened three times now.

Q: What direction was it pointing her in? At first, she wasn't sure. The next day, she mentioned the phrase to me and asked if I knew where it was from or what it meant. I recognized it and told her it was from a poem in the *Lord of the Rings*:

All that is gold does not glitter,
Not all those who wander are lost.

She wasn't particularly a fan of *Lord of the Rings* or sci-fi/ fantasy, so it was even more incredible that this phrase called out to her. As for the meaning of the phrase, well that was up to her. She realized that the message coming through was that it was OK to rent for a while longer, to "wander" rather than putting down roots by buying a house.

A few years later, she decided to move to California and was glad she hadn't bought a place in Arizona, because the market had crashed. Had she had a mortgage, it was unlikely she would have been able to move so easily.

The "errant phrase" is a great type of clue. It can be on a bumper sticker on a car, but more often it will jump out of the page at you while you are reading a book, surfing the web, looking at your email, or walking into a library or bookstore.

Remember that clues are subjective and that we are all on our own personal treasure hunts. Each Treasure Map is different. The "invisible hand" of the inner mentor will point out things in the environment that are important, and the "inner compass" will steer you in the direction of the clue through your feelings.

CASE STUDY NO. 13:

A Big Clue: Listening to the Inner Voice to Move and Start a Business

Sometimes it can be tough to listen to what a clue is saying when logic is telling us the opposite. It's important that we learn to balance the Left and Right Brain approaches so that we can confidently follow our intuition. Usually, when a clue is telling us to make a move from a job or a city, it is what I call a "Big Clue," because it is indicating you need to make a big change.

Jennifer was working in Boston with a staff job as a

photographer for The Community Newspaper Company, which included the *Boston Tab* and *Cambridge Tab*. In the photography world, this was considered a very good thing, because staff jobs are few and far between (many photographers work freelance, with an unsteady income stream). So logic told her she should be happy to have such a steady-paying job.

Sometimes, random people would call the newspaper asking it to cover their wedding (in the documentary style used by newspapers). Jenn started to do wedding photography herself at weekends and found she really enjoyed it. Unlike her work for the newspaper, in which she typically had only five to fifteen minutes for taking pictures, she found that wedding photography gave her a sense of connection with the people she was photographing. The work was *meaningful* in a way that her day job wasn't.

After noticing this disconnect between what she was doing at the weekends compared to what she was doing during the week, Jenn also realized she wasn't feeling "at home" in Boston any more. An inner voice told her: "Leave your job and move back to Austin, where you might be able to do wedding photography more regularly."

Logic told her that this wasn't a good idea—she had a great job and loved the colleagues she worked with in Boston, whereas she had no job at all in Austin. She didn't even know of a single wedding she could photograph there. What would she do for income in the meantime?

Jennifer says: "Somehow it felt like the right thing to do." She couldn't explain exactly why, but felt compelled to follow her intuition.

Sometimes, intuition comes from an inner voice telling us to do something that we feel strongly we should do, even though logic might tell us not to do it. When we want to do something that we can't explain, this can cause stress and anxiety in our lives—and Jenn's situation was no different.

After getting the message again and again, Jenn decided to follow her intuition: she quit her job and moved back to Austin. "I was anxious but I also felt compelled to do it—it was almost as if I didn't have a choice—that's how strong the intuition was around this. I couldn't ignore my feelings any longer."

As she contemplated what she would do next, Jenn knew she wanted to do only high-end weddings that could sustain her, and not take random photography jobs. But this would require her to have some funding, not just for her equipment, but to set up shop, to travel around the country for "high-end weddings," and she needed to support herself in the meantime.

Things happened quickly after Jennifer made her decision to move back to Austin. When she got back, within a week she met with an old friend and former college professor for lunch (Tacos!), who signed on to become her business partner, helping to establish her new business. She wanted to do more "natural" pictures rather than the traditional "posed" wedding pictures. He trusted her intuition and helped to establish her as Jennifer Lindberg Weddings (www.jenniferlindbergweddings.com).

About Big Clues

This example brings us to a specific kind of clue: an inner voice that needs no interpretation and is telling us we need to make a change in our life. In traditional cultures, this kind of "Big Clue" is one that demands to be followed. How can you be sure it's the right thing to do to make a change? Usually, we start by ignoring it with logical reasons, just like Jenn did, but then it builds up to a boiling point and we are compelled to make a change.

TREASURE HUNTING RULE NO. 7:

Sometimes a Big Clue will require no interpretation

How can you be sure that a clue is a Big Clue and that you should follow it? The key is in the feelings, which like a symphony building up to a crescendo, grow stronger and stronger with each note.

Paradoxically, sometimes the best advice to someone who is feeling the pull to do something is to ignore it, for a while. This is the same advice I give many entrepreneurs who think they want to quit their job and start a company doing X. Ignore it. At least for a little while.

Usually, if the calling is really a part of their personal life-spanning Treasure Map, they won't be able to ignore it for long. The voice will come back, stronger than ever, and they will feel themselves increasingly occupied with the idea, thinking about it day and night. That's the clue that this really is a Big Clue—the pressure builds up internally and you find that you "have to do it."

I call this the point of "No Choice." Just as Jennifer, after a while, felt that she had no choice but to move back to Austin and focus on her wedding photography, many entrepreneurs feel that they can't ignore an idea any longer but are compelled to jump in. They can ignore the idea for a little while but then no longer. Eventually, it's time to act on the clue, and once you do, it will lead you to the next clue.

CASE STUDY NO. 14:
A Trail of Lindens in the Virtual World

Another story from my start-up experiences illustrates when a clue is simply a nudging to "pay attention" to someone. We have all had the experience of walking into a room or a meeting or group of people and feeling drawn to learn more about one particular person.

When I was at Stanford Business School, I was thinking of attending a class on entrepreneurship that required the formation of a team of co-founders. I wasn't 100 percent sure about the class or who I would have as a team of co-founders, but I decided to put out feelers to see who else might be interested in a new technology area, "virtual worlds" such as *Second Life*, which was like an online multi-player game.

I liked the idea of a virtual world where people went and built virtual 3D landscapes and communities, and had a virtual economy that was driven by a virtual currency. The company that had made *Second Life* was called Linden Labs, and they had a virtual currency called Lindens.

I had just done a research paper about the price fluctuations of the virtual currency ("Lindens") and it was very much on my mind as I organized a lunch for other students from Stanford Business School who were interested in virtual worlds and gaming, to see if any of them wanted to take the entrepreneurship class and be part of a team.

There were probably five or six of us at the lunch, and we were just getting started when one of the students said that he really wanted me to meet one of his other friends, who he had also invited to the lunch. The name of his other friend was Lee Linden.

I was amused at the coincidence—I had organized a lunch thinking about *Second Life*, made by Linden Labs, and here was a guy that I hadn't invited but who was showing up named "Linden."

I got a funny, unusual feeling when I saw this coincidence. By itself, it might have meant nothing. I could've noticed it but then forgotten about it.

But because it seemed like a "clue," I decided to get to know Lee Linden better. It turned out he had started a mobile game company with his high school buddy, Ben, both of whom had grown up in Michigan (like me).

It was later, after we started working together, that I decided to become an investor in their company, Tapjoy, and subsequently I joined the board of directors. Tapjoy was a mobile gaming company that later became one of the largest mobile advertising companies, and both Lee and Ben went on to become some of the most successful entrepreneurs in Silicon Valley, selling their next company to Facebook. Not only was Tapjoy a good investment, but it got me started in the world of mobile gaming, and I would go on to co-found Gameview Studios, creators of *Tap Fish*, one of the most successful free-to-play games in the early days of mobile gaming.

Clues are like that. They are usually just "inklings" that you should pay attention to someone or something. It is up to you to do the follow-up, taking a half-step—in this case getting to know my new friend, Lee Linden, better. It took additional time for me to make decisions about investing in his company, but this shows how following your intuition in the form of a clue about a person can lead to a fruitful business relationship.

CASE STUDY NO. 15:

All Clues Point to Snickers!

Jack worked for a technology firm in Texas, and sat down after a long morning of interviewing candidates for their opening. It was into the afternoon and he hadn't had lunch yet. He remarked to his co-worker, "Man, I wish I had a Snickers bar or something right now," but there was no time in between interviews to get anything.

The next candidate that walked in, let's call him Henry, happened to mention, unprompted, that he'd picked up a Snickers bar but wasn't going to eat it. Instead, he offered it to Jack.

This made an impression on Jack, who rarely if ever eats Snickers bars and definitely never had a candidate spontaneously offer one to him. It was unusual and coincidental enough for Jack to wonder if perhaps they'd found their ideal candidate.

Was it unusual? Yes it was. *Did it repeat?* Yes, the Snickers bar started off being an internal thought, which Jack mentioned to his co-worker, and within an hour someone showed up and not only mentioned Snickers, but also had one with him.

This would definitely qualify as a clue, using our definition. What was the clue telling Jack? While we can't say for certain at this point whether Henry was the right person for the job, the *clue* was definitely pointing to Henry, as if saying, "Pay attention to this guy!"

At the end of the day, as Jack and his colleagues weighed the candidates, they decided that another candidate, let's call him Ben, had the most experience for the job, though Henry, the Snickers candidate, came a close No. 2. Despite Jack's intuition about Henry, logic told him that he should go along with Ben, who was "more qualified." After offering Ben the job, he reluctantly called up Henry to thank him for interviewing and passed on the news that he wasn't selected.

A few weeks later, just as Ben was supposed to start the new job, he called to cancel, saying that he'd had second thoughts about relocating to Texas. Jack quickly called up Henry, the Snickers candidate, who was still available and enthusiastic about the job.

What Happens When You Ignore a Clue

This story is one of many examples of someone recognizing a clue but deciding not to proceed in the direction it was pointing to, only later to realize that circumstances had rearranged themselves to make the clue more relevant than ever, which is our next Rule of Treasure Hunting:

TREASURE HUNTING RULE NO. 8:

Ignoring a clue may prove futile

This happens often, particularly when we let our "logical" conscious mind talk us out of going down the path of a particular clue.

We'll talk more about "where" clues come from in Chapter 10, "Where Do Clues Come From? A Spiritual and Religious Perspective" and Chapter 11, "Where Do Clues Come From? A Scientific Perspective," but it seems that they sometimes come from a place that has a broader view of what's going to happen in our work and lives—often seeing beyond circumstances or obstacles which appear to be permanent but are actually temporary.

In the next chapter, I'll give an example of a "Big Dream" which pointed out a product to me that my start-up should build. I ignored it, only to find our company, many months later, going down that path anyway!

This is why it's important to pay attention to clues, even if you are skeptical of them at first. If you notice a clue, then it may play a role in a larger pattern that you cannot see initially. The dots may not connect until some unknowable point in the future.

Let's look at another example of this.

CASE STUDY NO. 16:

The Universe Has Other Plans

When Arlene was a law school student in the early 1980s, she tried to get a legal internship in Seattle by sending a mailing to 50 law firms there. Arlene really wanted to go to Seattle because she had done a junior year abroad in Victoria, British Columbia, and she would be only about 50 miles away from her friends there.

One firm from Seattle told her that they were interested, but the hiring partner wanted to meet her in person before making a decision and she asked Arlene to wait until her next visit to the east coast. As Arlene waited, she was worried that the best opportunities were quickly disappearing, so she decided to call the hiring partner and told her she needed a commitment.

The partner said she needed to speak with her colleagues. When she got back to Arlene she told her that the decision would have to be "no" if she needed a decision right away.

Besides the 50 letters to Seattle, Arlene had applied for only one other job—a law firm in North Carolina. When they offered her the job initially, Arlene was still thinking in her "logical" mind that she wanted to go to Seattle, so said she was waiting to hear from other places before she decided. When the Seattle firm said no, Arlene went ahead and accepted the offer in North Carolina.

Arlene says: "I got off the phone after accepting the job and went to my next class. When I got out of class, there was a message on the job board that the Seattle people had changed their mind and offered me the job. I was torn because I really missed my friends in BC and had put so much effort into trying to develop a job there. On the other hand, I had given my word to the NC firm and that was not something I took lightly. I decided to keep my word. It was one of the best decisions I have ever made in my life!"

It turned out that the North Carolina job was with living legal legends. The head of the firm was Julius Chambers, a famous civil rights lawyer who'd won eight cases before the U.S. Supreme Court, including some well-known cases of racial integration and employment law, helping to change the face of history in so doing. This internship gave Arlene the chance to be on the cutting edge of civil rights cases, and being in North Carolina changed her life for the better in many ways.

This was a perfect example where the logical mind thinks, "I want X," but the clues are pointing us somewhere else. As much as we try to resist, we can eventually get the message. Arlene believes that going to North Carolina was a part of her Treasure Map, and it took the clues of getting "rejections" from the 49 law firms in Seattle for her to accept the job in North Carolina.

CASE STUDY NO. 17:

Following an Impulse into the Film Industry

Sometimes a totally unexpected clue emerges when you follow a random impulse that seems to have no logical reason behind it.

When I was in Arizona in 2006, I was driving south toward Tucson. I saw a sign that mentioned Native American souvenirs off the next exit of the freeway.

Now, in certain parts of Arizona this is a pretty common. I really wasn't in the mood to buy any Native American jewelry or tourist souvenirs, and I didn't need to use the rest room, but I decided to stop anyway on an impulse. There was just one little store with a rest room.

I looked around at the items being sold in the store, but none caught my eye. I decided to buy a bottle of water, concluding that my stopping at that particular exit was indeed just a random impulse rather than anything more meaningful.

As I was paying for my bottle of water, I noticed a little free newspaper, one of the Native American tribal newspapers (it might have been the *Navajo Times*, I can't recall now). On the cover was a story about a group of young men who were making a movie on the Navajo reservation.

I had a tingling sensation in my forehead when I saw that headline and paper. I picked it up and brought it with me into the car. Later, I read the article about a young man, Travis, an Iraq war veteran, who had lived on the Navajo reservation and, along with his friends, was casting for a movie called *Turquoise Rose*.

I had a funny feeling that I needed to find out more about these guys. Although I'd always had an interest in film and in Native American culture, this was the first time I had felt drawn to them both together. I had just sold my last company, and was trying to decide what to do next.

I contacted Travis and his friends and discovered that they were trying to raise money for their film. Though he was not Navajo, Travis had spent several years on the reservation. Then, when he had been deployed to Iraq, he'd thought of the idea and screenplay for the film. When he returned, he went to film school, and now he was trying to get this, his first independent feature film, off the ground.

I could tell from their business plan that they were going to have a hard time making this film with the budget they were looking at. While Travis had an interesting idea, this was his first film, and the projections, like most first-time business plans, looked a little rosy to me. I could also tell that the group weren't having much success in fund-raising.

I kept in touch with them and eventually decided that Travis, although he was a filmmaker, was also an entrepreneur, and I had invested in entrepreneurs before, so I decided to go ahead and invest in his little film project and became executive producer on my first film.

This was an interesting clue because it helped to launch both my career and Travis's as an independent filmmaker. It all started on a random impulse.

Over the years, I have learned to follow my impulses, particularly to stop and explore some place or area when I'm driving. This isn't always practical of course; if you are on a deadline or running late, for example. But over time you can learn the feeling of an "impulse" that you might want to follow.

CASE STUDY NO. 18:

Searching for Alternative Financing: A String of Clues

Let's take another business example from my own career. A few years back, I was contemplating raising venture capital financing for a new business that I had started up.

During this contemplation period, I had a dream, which I didn't remember fully, except that I recalled having a conversation about "royalty-based financing," which is a very different, non-standard model for financing companies. It's not quite equity investing (which is usually done through venture capitalists, who take an ownership share in the company) and it's not quite debt financing (which is usually done through banks; though they have no ownership of the company, they call all the shots because debt-holders get paid first, before anyone else).

I woke up and thought about the dream. I had looked into royalty financing almost a year before this dream happened as an "alternative" to venture capitalist financing—which has both a big upside and a big downside, and which has got me into trouble before. At that time, royalty financing was something the "invisible hand" had pointed out to me—something I was intrigued by and had the "odd sensation" might be important to me someday. But as often happens, I had become busy and forgotten all about it.

When the dream happened, I gave the idea some thought again, but decided to dismiss it in relation to the current business, again "for practical reasons." On the one hand, I decided my co-founders in the venture probably wouldn't want to do royalty financing because of how it might affect our ability to raise more capital down the road, and given the size of our company, the amount of money we could get from this funding source were very slim. So once again I "passed" on the clue.

Note that I went through the *intuition* stage initially (the "funny feeling" when I looked into royalty financing) a year earlier, and the "confirmation" stage (the dream) a year later. The interpretation of what it was implying seemed to be clear (attempt to raise "royalty-based financing"), but as I brought the Left Brain into the mix, I rejected that course of action and promptly forgot about it again.

This is very common, and you may find yourself doing this with your own Book of Clues. To "pass" and "not act" on a clue should be a conscious decision; usually you are saying, "Right now I don't think this is right, but I'll let it go and see if it comes up again."

Within a week or two of my dream, I found myself randomly popping open one of my old notebooks. It opened to a page on which I had written some notes on royalty-based financing, including the phone number of a guy who used to have a fund that did this, and the website address of what he had said was a "new fund" in Maine looking to make investments. I had forgotten that I'd even made these notes!

This kind of repetition is exactly what leads to taking a clue more seriously. Once again I considered this option, looking at the website, but once again I came to the conclusion that (1) our company wouldn't fit their criteria—they wanted larger companies with larger revenues, and (2) my co-founders wouldn't go for it. So once more I let it go, deciding not to take any action.

Within a week or two, I found myself emptying my

briefcase, and a red folder jumped out at me from among my pile of old folders. I picked it out, opened it up, and guess what it contained? A set of brochures on royalty financing that I had collected a year earlier.

I began to "reflect" on this set of synchronicities. It was enough to convince me that I should at the very least look into this "alternate" source of financing. And then it hit me that, whether or not we went for royalty financing, this was really a "clue" telling me that we should consider "alternate" funding sources, rather than simply going down the "standard" road of venture capital.

This interpretation seemed to make sense to me, and I resolved to go ahead and investigate these sources.

Within a few days of this reflection, I opened my email and among the hundreds of "spam" or "junk" email message that I get each day was one that I had never seen before but that caught my attention. It read: "How venture capital ruined my company" and it was an ad for someone who had written a book on the dangers of venture capital financing.

I knew this all too well, as I had lived that story. I didn't buy the book, but took it as a *confirmation* and *reflection* of my recognition that I had understood the clue: look at alternative sources of financing.

CASE STUDY NO. 19:
Finding Shamanic Journeying and a Mentor
While I was attending a workshop in Miami, a very casual conversation with someone about my interest in dreams led them to make two suggestions to me: that I look into

classes on "shamanism and dreamwork," and that I read a specific book, an ancient Chinese tale translated as *Monkey: Journey to the East.*

This "casual" conversation left me with that "funny feeling" of the "invisible hand" at work, and so I decided to follow up on both suggestions. (As an interesting follow-on, the person who made these suggestions to me dropped out of the classes shortly after our conversation in Miami and I never saw them again.)

When I got back to Boston, I found myself having to go to Gloucester, a fishing town north of Boston on Cape Ann, because I had received a parking ticket that summer in Rockport, a well-known tourist town on Cape Ann. I had to take the train up to the country magistrate and pay my fine. Since I had some time to wait before the next train, I decided to stop at a bookstore between the courthouse and the train station to see if they had this book called "Monkey." I found a second-hand bookstore just around the corner from the courthouse, and though they did not have the book, the proprietor offered to order it for me.

Because he was a talkative fellow and I liked the feel of the bookstore, I asked what other books he might have on this subject. The only book on "dreams" he had was called *Conscious Dreaming* and though I wasn't familiar with the name of the author at that time, I bought it and took it back with me to my place in Boston.

Following up on my other "tip" from the Miami trip, I then went home and decided to do a search on the internet for "Shamanic Dreaming" to see if there was anyone close by who offered such classes. I found someone named

Robert Moss in Albany, and thought that might be close enough to drive to the classes, as I could find nothing in the Boston area. I registered for a class via email.

I then went back to read more of the book I had just bought—*Conscious Dreaming*. It wasn't until a few hours later that I looked again at the name of the author and realized it was written by Robert Moss—the same person whose name I had just found on the internet and who I had made arrangements to attend a class with.

I thought this was *enough* of a coincidence to merit me writing it down. As I went to my bookshelf to put the book away, I noticed a black book that I remembered buying in *Rockport*, on *Cape Ann*, a few years earlier, but hadn't read. It gave me a "funny feeling" but I ignored it. Later that night, I took out the black book and looked at the name of the author—and lo and behold it was the same Robert Moss!

This was a case where a single author had come up three times in a single day! I decided it was definitely worth taking the action of driving all the way to Albany to attend his classes.

The themes of *shamanic journeying, Rockport* and *dreams* were playing out in this pattern, and Robert Moss became a mentor of mine for many years, and encouraged me to write this current book about synchronicity and dreams.

Once again, here we see an example of a pattern unfolding and revealing itself over time, with multiple coincidental experiences piling up on one another. In my case, these clues involved the convergence over years of several threads in my own personal *tapestry*, of business, dreaming, spirituality and writing. By following the clues when they were in "on" mode, and simply "biding my time" when they were in off mode, I allowed the threads to show themselves and to be woven in this particular way.

Waking Up to the Stream of Clues

This chapter has given several examples of what I call the "stream of clues" that come to us throughout the day. It's important to learn to pay attention to your feelings, which are the key to determining if something is a clue. This "stream of clues" is coming in constantly—while you are awake and even while you are asleep (which we'll explore).

The key is to pay attention to your feelings, and to ask the treasure-hunting questions:

- Is it unusual?
- Does it repeat?
- What does it mean to me?
- What direction is it pointing me in?

If you keep the Clue Lifecycle in mind the whole time, you'll see yourself moving seamlessly from one stage to the next. As you move from intuition to confirmation (repetition of the clue), you can then interpret and take action, which will lead you to the next clue (validation).

If you are having trouble picking up on this stream of clues, you can try some of the following exercise to start opening yourself up to this stream.

EXERCISE

Go Clue-hunting

Sometimes, you can simply engage in an activity and see what the "Invisible Hand" and your "Inner Compass" point out to you. Here are several activities you can do to deliberately start looking for clues:

1   Go into a bookstore or library and see what titles draw your attention. It is very possible that your eyes will be drawn to a specific title of a book on a shelf. This title could be an "errant" phrase. You might not even need to read the book—the title or subtitle of a book can be enough to jog your internal compass that there is a clue there.

2   Clean up your desk/room to get unstuck. Earlier I gave the example of being stuck on my new manuscript, so I decided to clean my room. This is actually a great exercise which gets the energy moving when you feel "stuck" in your work or your "job" or just your life. There is the physical act of cleaning up, but also the freeing of energy that may be trapped in the clutter you have in your room or on your desk at work. More importantly, during this process you can see what draws your attention. In my case, it was an old manuscript of my first book with scribbles on it. In another instance, it was a folder about "alternative financing." In another, it was a book of dreams.

3   Go to an event and see who or what the "invisible
    hand" points out to you. Of course, going to a
    conference, gathering or meetup can be interesting
    if you are into the topic, but the idea here is to see
    what people in the audience, or waiting outside the
    door, or at a party at the conference, your mind is
    drawn to. Pay attention to uncanny feelings and
    inner sensations. It could be a latecomer to the
    gathering, or it might be someone you are standing
    next to in line.

4   Drive to a nearby suburb or city that you've been
    to before, but without a specific purpose. Wander
    around for a bit, have some coffee and drive back.
    What do you notice that you haven't noticed before
    about this city or on the drive? If it's unusual,
    particularly if it's in a place you have been to before
    but never noticed, then it might be a clue!

In all of these cases, the idea is not just to engage in the
activity, but to flex your intuitive muscles while you are
fully awake. See who or what you are drawn to naturally.
Don't force it. Follow it. Pay attention to your feelings,
and only then will you start to notice the steady stream of
clues that your inner mentor is sending you.

"There is little difference between the intuitions of primitive peoples and ourselves. The dreams and visions that were given to the wise ones, the medicine people and prophets of old, are also available to us."

–Tom Brown
Field Guide to Living with the Earth

CHAPTER 5

Big Dreams and Little Messages

What Do Dreams Have to Do with Business?

In this chapter, I'd like to focus on a certain type of clue, one that most of us in the West are trained to ignore: our dreams. What do dreams have to do with your career or business?

After all, living in the business world is about marshaling of resources, producing goods and services to meet the needs of the market, and building and managing complex organizational structures.

If we take a broader view of business, then we're talking about broad economic cycles, interest rate fluctuations, stock market prices, etc. If we take a more personal view, then we're concerned with our career, the finding of a suitable job, promotions, salary, job qualifications, etc.

Surprisingly, *all of these areas* can be affected by, and in turn do affect, our dreams.

I have found that dreams are far more than weird pictures we see when we're asleep—they can be used to bring through specific information that can be of value to us in our personal and professional lives. This can range from decisions made about where to go to college, whether to accept a specific job, or even, in my own case, what products to build for a new start-up.

This book contains numerous historical examples of how dreams and visions have been the inspiration for many of our great scientific and political achievements of the past few hundred years. This chapter will focus specifically on "Big Dreams," and the next chapter will focus on everyday dreams, or what we might affectionately call "little dreams."

Big Dreams and Little Dreams: a Cultural Perspective

Many cultures around the world, ranging from the Tibetans in Asia, the Aborigines in Australia, Arabic cultures in the Middle East, and many Native American cultures, placed a great deal of importance on dreams as a source of guidance and insight. They all placed particular emphasis on a type of dream—what is often referred to by different names as a Big Dream.

Tibetan Buddhists, for example, believe that dreams can be divided into meaningful dreams (which they refer to as *dreams of clarity*) and everyday dreams (which they call *ordinary karmic dreams*, because they seem to regurgitate the events of the day). In the Tibetan view, ordinary karmic dreams are of very little benefit to us—we often forget them, or remember only bits and fragments of them, but the dreams of clarity are very important to our personal development and are in fact a signpost on the road to enlightenment.

Most of our everyday dreams might fit into the bucket of "little" dreams—dreams that are concerned with what happened to us on that day, or seemingly random dreams that have no particular structure, meaning or coherency.

Some Western psychologists believe that these "little" dreams reveal much of value about our current psychological state and the issues we are wrestling with. We'll explore ways to work with daily dreams in Chapter 6, "Clues that Come in the Night: Everyday Dreams and Synchronicity."

In many Native American cultures, such as the Iroquois

and Sioux, Big Dreams were considered important enough that the direction of an entire tribe might be determined by a dream that brought through specific information and guidance about the future. The Maricopa Indians of the American southwest believed that almost everything that happens to us in waking life happens in a dream first.

So important was "dreaming" to Native American cultures that an individual who had a "Big Dream" might have his name chosen in honor of that dream. An example of this is the Sioux warrior and chief named "Crazy Horse," who gave the Native Americans one of their few victories over the white settlers during the Indian Wars of the nineteenth century in the now famous battle of Little Bighorn.

Many today think that this name reflects the way he fought, but that isn't exactly right. When he was young, the boy who later became known as Crazy Horse had a dream vision of the "other world" which he described as being "behind this world." In this dream, he was on a horse that moved back and forth in a wild manner while he lobbed arrows as a mighty warrior. He cited the "energy" of this dream as developing his ability to wage and win battles. His name, "Crazy Horse," was given to him because of how his horse acted in this particular vision.

But Big Dreams weren't reserved only for chiefs and leaders of wars. Often, a young adult would be taught to incubate a dream or vision over a course of several days. When the dream or vision came, it would sometimes reveal not only a name that the dreamer would be known by, but also a glimpse of a life path for that individual to follow—as a warrior, as a healer.

If we were to look at this in today's terms, we might say that young adults in Native American cultures used their dreams to find and progress along their chosen *career paths*.

Let's start with two Big Dreams that are still affecting the world to this day, though most of us probably haven't heard of them.

CASE STUDY NO. 20:

A Big Dream, the Federation and the Constitution

One such Big Dream occurred several hundred years ago to a young man named Deganawidah and resulted in a sophisticated political system, referred to as the League of the Iroquois, which continues to affect us today.

Before that time, the related tribes that later became known as the Iroquois Confederacy—the Mohawk, Oneida, Onondaga, Cayuga and Seneca—were constantly at war with each other. As a result of this infighting, they were constantly weak when attacked by other surrounding tribes.

Deganawidah woke up one morning and had a particularly vivid dream. In the dream, he saw a mighty tree of "Great Peace." When he looked at the roots of this great tree, he saw that each of the strong roots that anchored the tree represented one of the five nations. When he awoke, he realized that the dream was calling on him to forge a new alliance between the five nations that would make them much stronger together than they were individually.

In many Native American cultures, a Big Dream was a wake-up call from the spirits that showed the way not only for the dreamer, but also perhaps for the whole tribe.

Deganawidah did exactly that—he followed his dream. Along with his disciple Hiawatha, he went from tribe to tribe to create that alliance of "Great Peace" which he had dreamed about. Eventually, this resulted in a novel political structure; the five nations were bound together by a "federal" system, called the League of the Iroquois, which formed an early experiment in democracy. The federal "governing council" was only responsible for matters that would affect the entire League, and left tribal matters to be decided individually by the nations.

This proved to be a remarkably effective system, as it freed the different nations from warring with each other, and resulted in the ability to consolidate resources to defend the League from outsiders.

When the founding fathers of the United States of America, including Benjamin Franklin and Thomas Jefferson, were looking for a model on which to base the new "Union," they didn't have to look very far. They not only noted but also *explicitly borrowed* from the structure of the League of the Iroquois, a "federal" government that dealt only with issues that affected the whole Union, and reserved all other areas to be "determined by the states."

This is a story that deserves a little more attention in our history books than we give it. Deganawidah had a Big Dream, which provided a vision of a complex political system that affected the direction of not only his own path in life, but also the lives of all the Iroquois. In fact, through the United States Constitution, partly based on the structure inspired by the Tree of Great Peace, Deganawidah's dream is still affecting us to this day.

CASE STUDY NO. 21:
A Big Dream and the Call to Prayer

Our next Big Dream takes us back even further, to approximately AD 600, when the Prophet Muhammad was introducing Islam into Arabia. It was said that the first revelation of the Qur'an came to Muhammad while he was sleeping in a cave outside Mecca, from the angel Gabriel. Whether that was a dream or a waking vision is a source of confusion, but one cannot doubt its importance in shaping the Middle East and the world.

However, the Big Dream that I want to relay here is one of a more practical nature, and perhaps one of the earliest recorded instances of both "incubating a dream" and "mutual dreaming" (where two or more people have the same dream). This concerns the origins of the "Azan," or call to prayer. Anyone who has been to a Middle Eastern country will have heard this call to prayer, which is recited five times a day over loudspeakers in every major Muslim city.

After Muhammad had moved from his birth city of Mecca to the nearby city of Medina, the new religion was starting to catch on and the number of followers was growing.

The story, as told by one of the Prophet's first followers, Abu Umayr, was that Muhammad was looking for a way to call his followers to prayer. Since clocks were not available, and the new religion required praying five times a day, this was no small issue.

Some of his followers suggested raising a flag, or using a horn, or a bell, but Muhammad noted that the Christians of the time used a bell, and the Jews used a horn, and a flag wasn't obvious enough.

Another of his first followers, Abdullah ibn Zayd, was with the Prophet during this exchange and was anxious to find an answer. Later that night, he had a dream, or a dream vision in between wakefulness and sleep, in which someone came in and taught him the call to prayer. The Prophet took this to be divine guidance and the Azan was born.

A few weeks after Abdullah ibn Zayd had mentioned the dream to the Prophet, another early disciple of Muhammad, Umar ibn al Khattab, revealed that he had heard a similar "call to prayer" in a dream a few weeks earlier but had failed to mention it since it was only a dream. There was the confirmation needed, and they adopted it as the "call to prayer" for the new religion. From that day forward, the Azan, first glimpsed in two separate dreams, became the call that has been heard every day now for over a thousand years in cities around the world.

Can You Have a Big Dream Today?

It's all well and good, you might think, for Native American and Middle Eastern prophets to rely on their dreams, but of what value are such dreams today?

This book is to remind us that we too can still have Big Dreams and today. They can reveal specific guidance on issues and matters of great importance to our jobs, our careers, and they can reveal the "wishes of our soul."

How can you tell if you've had a Big Dream?

While to Native Americans it was obvious when a dream was important enough to be considered a Big Dream, I would define a Big Dream today as simply a dream that has a significant impact on your life or career. This could be in a psychological way, because it deals with an important issue in your personal life; or in a professional way, because it gives you guidance on a specific path that is right for you to follow; or in a spiritual way, because it inspires you by leaving you with a feeling of sacredness; or perhaps in *all of these ways* at once.

It was the arrival of a number of Big Dreams like this in my own life that brought through specific information related to my career path and business choices. Eventually, as these dreams were validated, I became convinced that dreams could be a source of credible and valuable wisdom and guidance.

Because, like most Westerners, I was taught not to pay attention to "dreams," this evolution in my own thinking about dreams took longer than it otherwise might have done. In many cases, I often noted a Big Dream but didn't do anything about it for a long time, only to find that events in my professional life and in the business world rearranged themselves to be consistent with my dream. After this happened several times, even a MIT-trained engineer like myself could no longer deny that dreams, particularly Big Dreams could be important clues to help us navigate our life and career.

CASE STUDY NO. 22:
A Big Dream for a Start-up

This was true of a dream I had in the fall of 2001, when I was contemplating starting a new business: I entered a very large, well-carpeted room. It looked like a ballroom at a hotel, complete with chandelier, bar and lots of little tables. In the room were mostly men (with a few women) dressed in business suits, milling around near tables which had cocktails and snacks on them. There was a lot of chatter, but not much in the way of animated conversation.

I noticed that everyone seemed to be very polite toward each other, in a detached way. It looked very much like a scene from many conferences I had been to—but I couldn't read any badges to help me make out which conference it was. I walked up to a group of middle-aged men, all dressed in suits, and recognized one of them—James, who had been a mentor of mine in my early career.

The men welcomed me, and I asked them what businesses they were into these days, now that the internet bubble had burst. "We're all into XML nowadays," said one of them. "Yes, that's what I recommend, get into XML," said another. James simply smiled. "Are all of you into XML?" I asked, and got nodded agreements. Suddenly they all seemed to jump into conversation with each other and ignored me.

I looked in my hand. There was a piece of glossy paper, like a product brochure. I turned it over and on it was a picture that resembled a spider web of connections. In the middle was a circle with XML written within it. On the left were some other formats—I couldn't quite tell what they were. And on the right-hand side, on the top and bottom, there were other boxes.

I looked at the picture and it looked familiar. I said in my mind, "This looks like DataLink," which was a product that tied together different systems from my previous start-up. "Except, this uses a new technology, XML," I said. The rest of the group that I had been talking to were continuing their conversation, ignoring me.

And then I woke up. The dream had a "certain quality" about it that made me think about it long and hard. It felt like a significant dream and I had no problem remembering it the next day, or weeks, months, even years afterwards.

What Happens When You Don't Follow a Big Dream

At this time, the great internet bubble of the late 1990s had burst, and I wasn't sure about what kind of business to start next. Being a software engineer, I was naturally looking at different computer-related technologies to find the next "big thing." A technology called "XML," a universal format for the storage of almost any type of information, had caught my attention. But I hadn't been thinking of using this technology in the way that the dream revealed. At the time, I was partial to using this technology for a different kind of product, one that would be used by companies to monitor their competitors' websites, so I didn't follow this dream.

A few months into this new business, we determined that perhaps the approach we were taking to building our product wasn't going to work; now, we needed to create a different product using some of the work we'd done to date.

As we looked around for a pivot, we found ourselves building a product that looked surprisingly similar to the one drawn in the brochure in my dream. We used XML as the "middle man" to many different document formats, and in the end our drawings that described the product in our brochures looked very much like the "spider" in my dream. We also found that XML was still one of the few "hot" areas in the technology sector at that time, even after most other internet-related technologies had "faded."

In other words, the events in my professional life had rearranged themselves so that the guidance in the dream became very useful.

About Big Dreams: Prophecy, Symbolism and More

Was the dream prophetic? Or had the dream merely given me the idea that I should move the company in a particular direction, making it a self-fulfilling prophecy? Or was the dream simply my unconscious putting together pieces that I already knew about—XML, the internet bubble, document formats? Or was it some combination of these?

A strict Freudian may have looked for "wish fulfillment" in this dream. He could probably have found it—a "wish" to have a successful start-up built on some new technology. A Jungian might have looked for archetypes that my unconscious brought through in this dream. And there was at least one: the archetype of the "mentor" who gives advice at a much-needed time. Occultists might have said that I visited the astral plane and actually visited James and his friends, or actually saw the future. Other psychiatrists may have interpreted the dream in terms of my relationship to my career and business in general, and my emotions and feelings about it.

According to Jeremy Taylor, in his excellent book on dreams, *Where People Fly and Water Runs Uphill*, none of these interpretations by themselves can be ruled out. The dream could be interpreted in all of these ways *simultaneously* without invalidating any one of them. This is because of the complexity used in dream symbols, which we'll pick up on in later chapters.

Whatever the interpretation, certain Native American cultures would say simply that I had a Big Dream that called to be followed.

This Big Dream was to affect my career path in life by helping me define a product for my start-up. Native American cultures might also tell me that a Big Dream deserves to be followed through. Even if it isn't at first, we may find events in the world rearranging themselves in a way that makes the fulfillment of the Big Dream more likely.

> ## TREASURE HUNTING RULE NO. 9:
>
> Pay attention when you have a Big Dream

How can you learn to recognize Big Dreams of your own?

While there are no hard-and-fast rules, I have found that there are several characteristics that can help one to identify a Big Dream:

- **A Big Dream usually deals with the future, and may bring the past forward.** My dream dealt with the past, present and future simultaneously. It brought the *past* into play in two ways: the character James had been a mentor of mine when I started my first business many years before having this dream, and my remark that the product sheet looked like "DataLink" reflected the fact that this was an actual product that my previous start-up had developed. It dealt with the *present*— at the time I had this dream I was in a period of transition: I had just left a job and was contemplating starting a new business. And it dealt with the *future*, because it laid out some very concrete thoughts concerning where I might be and what area I might focus on for the next few years. Most importantly, it combined these elements in an interesting way.

- **A Big Dream usually deals with paths to take in your life.** If you have something that's been bothering you during the day, it's likely to show up in your dreams. In this example, my dream dealt very clearly with the issue of what to do next—the next step in my career path. I had been thinking very much about this, and that "incubated" the dream, just as Abdullah ibn

Zayd's concern over the Prophet Muhammad's request for a call to prayer incubated his dream. There's more on how to call forth Big Dreams in Chapter 9, "Problem Solving and Creativity from Dreams: Not Just for Old, Dead People."

- **A Big Dream usually has both literal and symbolic elements.** While many of our dreams are symbolic, other dreams can bring out very clear, "literal" information. I found that the clearer my dreams have become, the more literal the information becomes. We tend to remember our dreams as a jumble of non-sequential images, and so we usually fail to take them seriously. There were several recurring symbols in this dream for me personally—the "generic" business conference is a setting that appears in my dreams whenever there is a prophetic quality to my dreams about business. A character representing James, who was an early mentor of mine, shows up every so often in my dreams as well. There's more about recognizing and using symbols from dreams in Chapter 6, "Clues that Come in the Night: Everyday Dreams and Synchronicity."

- **A Big Dream has a certain, memorable quality to it.** While the memory of most dreams fades quickly upon waking up, Big Dreams tend to stay with us, and we notice things in our environment that remind us of these dreams. You don't have to worry so much about the normal problem of "I remembered the dream clearly when I woke up but then forgot it quickly" with Big Dreams. In my own case, though I wrote it down right away, I would remember it very clearly many months later. Different dreams have different qualities about them. It's important to recognize that the non-quantifiable elements that make up the "quality" of a dream can be clues—the texture of the landscape, the level of attachment that you have to the dream, the vividness of your memory of the dream, or the feeling that the dream leaves you with.

- **Big Dreams usually have confirmation from the world around you.** A Big Dream doesn't stand on its own. It usually brings in elements that you will see in your waking life in the days, weeks and months after the dream. When these elements appear in the outside world, you might experience a sense of *déjà vu*, which is one way to recognize that the dream has played itself out. In my dream about XML, this was certainly true. Soon after having the dream, I began to see XML all around me—in articles, from my friends in the software industry. Eventually, as we have seen, the dream played itself out in a very literal way; within six months I had started a company that was producing a product very similar to the one I had seen described in the dream. We'll explore the idea of synchronicity and dreams in the following chapter.

- **Big Dreams can help you to solve a problem that you've been wrestling with.** Sometimes, a Big Dream will present a solution to a problem that you've been wrestling with. A famous example comes from Elias Howe, the inventor of the sewing machine, which shows again how dreams can have an impact on the business world.

Howe was struggling with how to thread the needle in his new invention—he had tried different approaches, but they kept failing. Then one night he had a dream in which he was caught by a tribe of cannibals and put into a big cauldron of water. Needless to say, he was very nervous and frightened by this turn of events, so much so that he almost missed a very important clue from his dream: the natives had holes at the tip of their spears. As soon as he awoke, he realized that this was the solution to his engineering problem—by threading the needle at the tip, and not at the back end, he was able to get his invention to work.

Lest you think this is a rare case, Chapter 9, "Problem Solving and Creativity from Dreams: Not Just for Old, Dead People" contains numerous examples of how dreams have helped famous scientists, inventors and politicians to solve key problems they were wrestling with.

- **Big Dreams often bring out mentors and guides.** Sometimes, in a Big Dream, a mentor will appear who will give us advice. This doesn't have to be a physical person who's served as a mentor, but could be a fictional character or a universal archetype. The appearance of a mentor is used by our dream consciousness to get past the need for complex symbols that we need to interpret—the dream can tell us what we're looking for in the dream.
- **Big Dreams are very unique to the person dreaming them.** This might sound obvious, but Big Dreams don't necessarily follow one of the "basic, recurring"

types of dreams that psychiatrists love to analyze, such as "showing up on the first day of school without any clothes on," or "falling dreams." While those dreams are important in their own way, Big Dreams are much more unique and usually reveal something about the dreamer that is very personal to them and their career path. If you had a Big Dream about your career, it would most definitely be different from a Big Dream that I might have about my career. We will explore this theme of the unique way in which Big Dreams and little messages conspire to both reveal and allow you to follow the "wishes of your own soul" in Chapter 12, "The Tapestry Reveals Itself," and Chapter 13, "Injecting Soul into the Soul-less Machine."

- **Big Dreams call out to be followed in some way.**
  I learned the idea of "honoring a dream" from Robert Moss, who has studied Native American dreaming practices extensively and written about them in his books, starting with *Conscious Dreaming*. Honoring a dream is about bringing the energy of the dream into real life in some way. But Big Dreams don't just call to be honored—they call to be followed.

  You'll notice that in my own case, I didn't really do anything with this dream initially; in fact, I went in a very different direction with my new business. But because this was a "Big Dream," it called out to be followed and, sooner or later, I found myself honoring it by building the product that had been hinted at in the dream.

If you follow the techniques laid out in this book, you can start to incubate, call forth, recognize and act on Big Dreams in your own life and career path. While the guidance may be personal, in the case of both Deganawidah and Abdullah ibn Zayd (among countless others) Big Dreams were of tribal, societal and even universal importance.

CASE STUDY NO. 23:
To Run or Not to Run? A Presidential Dream

Sometimes Big Dreams can help you to make a decision. This can be a small decision or a life-changing one. One such Big Dream happened to Lyndon Johnson, when he was thinking of running for re-election in 1968, in the middle of the ever-increasing escalation of the Vietnam War.

He was in a bit of a bind, having escalated the Vietnam War yet wanting to emphasize the domestic programs of his presidency, such as the Civil Rights Act and the War on Poverty.

One night, he had a dream in which he was struggling in the sea between two shores and wasn't able to swim successfully to either shore. Before this dream, he had been extremely anxious about whether to run for re-election. After it, Johnson later wrote, he made his decision not to run again and slept "like a baby" the rest of the night.

This was a Big Dream not just for Johnson but also for the country. But Big Dreams can be "big" in your life and don't need to involve world-changing events, or even start-ups or business. They could simply involve a major decision you are trying to make. Let's look at an example.

CASE STUDY NO. 24:

Where to Go to College?

Annie, a high school senior in Rhode Island, had applied to several colleges in Providence and other locations, including Boston. She had been to Boston once or twice, but was unsure where to go for college.

One day, she woke up from a dream that was super-colorful. It had a "certain" quality to it that can't be described but had to be felt. In the dream, she was wandering around Boston with a super-colorful sky and she felt at peace and at home there. She saw herself walking around everywhere, including Faneuil Hall, a Boston landmark from the American revolution, and felt at home in a way that she had never felt in Rhode Island.

When she woke up, she remembered not just the content but the *energy* of the dream and how it made her feel. From that day forward, she decided she was going to go to school in Boston and ended up living there for many years afterwards. Whenever she tried to move to different cities in the country, she found that she always wanted to move back to Boston, because it was one of the most walkable cities in the country, a fact that she hadn't really known when she had the dream and made the decision.

CASE STUDY NO. 25:

Who Is the Greatest Healer?

Ji Hyang had the following dream when she was transitioning from academia to having her own healing practice. This definitely qualifies as a Big Dream, because it dealt with her personal doubts and her path in seeking teachers.

Ji said that the dream appeared "completely clear, in full detail, as if half of it were spoken to me, half of it seen." The dream went like this:

A young man of a village wishes to become a medicine man, or healer. He needs to find a healing teacher. From a wise person in the village, he receives a scrap of gold lamé fabric, and the words, "the greatest teacher will have exactly this fabric." So he sets out. Crosses river and mountain, from village to village. Everywhere he goes, he inquires into the healing arts. When he hears of a healer, he goes to find them, inquires with his scrap of gold lamé fabric, studies together with them for a bit, then moves on. As he makes his rounds, people of the village who know of his interest occasionally approach him with their maladies. When this takes place, he politely explains that he is not a healer, only a student, and that he is very dedicated to his search for this great teacher. Once he has found and studied with the great teacher, he will come back to heal them.

One day, a woman approaches him. Her child is sick. He begins to explain the situation: he is just a student, he is searching. "No," she says. "My child needs you now. He has a dangerously high fever. " So the young man goes to her house, to the child's bedside. He tries every remedy, every technique at his disposal. He pours every inner resource, all the energy of his body and mind, into the situation, his sweat mingling with the fever-sweat of the child. At the end of the night, the fever breaks. The first light of dawn illuminates the room: the child and young man lying together exhausted on the bed, and the child's receiving blankets, which are wrapped together with a swath of gold lamé fabric.

The young man has an awakening of insight: the great teacher, in fact, is the experience of pouring body and mind, all inner resources, completely into a situation. His heart, broken open by the experience, is able to receive the healing gift he had sought (healing light is drawn in and is able to radiate forth). Thus it is that to serve is also to receive teaching.

While this dream was about becoming a healer, which had particular significance for Ji Hyang and her life and career, there's a great lesson there for all of us as we pursue our life's work.

CASE STUDY NO. 26:

A Monster Dream for Job Seekers

Lest you think my Big Dream about a start-up is unique, let's end this chapter with another example of a well-known success that started with a dream.

Jeff Taylor was a Boston-area recruiter who one night had a particularly vivid dream. He had been working for a client who wanted a "big idea." Jeff thought he should come up not just with a big idea but with a "monster" idea.

On the night in question, he woke up from a dream in which he'd envisioned a website that would electronically connect job seekers with employers. The dream was unlike other dreams that Jeff had had, because of its vividness in detail—the structure of the website, even individual pages and workflow, appeared to Jeff in the dream.

When Jeff woke up, he knew that he had just experienced a Big Dream, because of the impression it had left on him. He immediately sat down and started sketching the different pages of the website, and over the next few weeks and months he worked diligently to bring this "dream vision" into reality.

The company that Jeff started was Monster.com, which went on to become one of the leading career sites on the net, both during the internet boom and after the subsequent bust. Jeff Taylor's dream eventually helped thousands, if not millions, of jobseekers to find the right job for them.

The Stuff that Dreams Are Made of

These last few examples, involving monumental decisions by a U.S. president, several start-ups, as well as personal decisions about going to school and becoming a healer, point out that the "feeling" a dream leaves you with is as important as the content of the dream itself. In Annie's college dream, the energy of the dream and how "at home" she felt in Boston was important in unlocking the clue. Similarly, how "conflicted" Johnson had been in the presidential dream about his inability to reach either shore was an important element. In the healing dream, the key was Ji Hyang's energy of claiming her own power as a healer.

While we may have a Big Dream only rarely, we have little dreams that may be bringing us messages on an almost daily basis. Dreams can be a mechanism for gaining self-knowledge that can be critical to us in our professional lives, or can reveal to us truths that we aren't directly able or willing to see.

Big Dreams are like Big Clues—they demand to be followed, and even if you don't follow them initially, they find a way to be heard. You don't have to write down a Big Dream and (usually) you don't even have to interpret it—such dreams usually represent "wishes of the soul" as some Native American traditions refer to them and they stay with us.

Little dreams, dreams that happen all the time, on the other hand, can be a confusing mishmash, difficult to remember and chock full of symbolism that needs to be unraveled. As the Talmud says, a dream un-interpreted is

like a letter that remains unopened. Let's take a look at
how to work with everyday dreams.

"When we find that the whole constellation of a number of dream things corresponds so exactly to a situation later met during waking life, the belief in a mere 'accident' is the most impossible of all hypotheses."

–Medard Boss

CHAPTER 6

Clues that Come in the Night: Everyday Dreams and Synchronicity

When Inner and Outer Events Collide

In the last few chapters, I have quoted many experiences that started out in a dream, and then either influenced or were confirmed by events in the physical world. I call these experiences *clues that come in the night*, and they are an important and central part of a lifelong treasure hunt.

For many years, even while there were many such synchronicities happening all around me, I was blissfully unaware of these clues, at least at a conscious level. As a MIT-trained engineer and a "respectable businessman," I was always looking for concrete "cause" and "effect" in life. If there was no apparent, *visible causality* between two distinct events (whether "inner" or "outer"), I didn't draw any conscious links between them.

It's not easy for most people to get out of the linear cause and effect to see that there are other ways of perceiving the world and other types of patterns. For me, the kicker was when I started to see things in my dreams that were confirmed later on by events in waking life, what we think of as the "real world" (as opposed to the "dream world").

This led me to an intense curiosity about dreams and how they worked. Dreams are one of the most studied phenomena in human history, and there are many theories about how they work. More books have probably been written about dreams than about almost any other subject, simply because of the fact that dreams are universal and humans have been having them and interpreting them since the dawn of time.

Scientists and mystics tell us the same thing: everyone dreams, even if they don't remember their dreams. So just where do dreams come from and what are they all about?

The theories range from "random neurons firing" to more "psychological" explanations such as wish fulfillment (Freud) or the playing out of archetypes (Jung), to more literal interpretations.

Some Native American traditions, such as the Maricopa Indians of the southwest, believed that dreams were "rehearsals" for events that would come in later life. Others believed that dreams are a platform for many psychic phenomena, including conversations with those that have passed on and are now on the other side. Some experts and ancient cultures believe that dreams are a way for our unconscious to process the day's events; for example, Tibetan Buddhists in particular, believe that everyday dreams arise from small karmic traces that we accumulate throughout our daily lives.

While many of these explanations for dreams may be true, the most important aspect of dreams from the point of view of your own personal treasure hunt is to work with your dreams to find clues in them, which can later be confirmed in waking life, and/or provide guidance on where to go for your next clue.

Let's start our discussion of dreams by focusing on a specific type of synchronicity—a situation where an element from a dream (an "inner" event) shows up in real life the next day (the "outer" event) without an apparent causal relationship.

A Famous Example from Jung

When Jung was first defining synchronicity he gave a famous example of a patient of his who was stuck in her therapy and having trouble moving forward. During their session, the patient described a dream to Jung that she'd had the night before, which included a golden scarab. Just at that moment, there was a tap on the window. Jung opened the window and a golden-green beetle (probably the closest to a scarab in Jung's part of the world, Switzerland) flew in.

This was a great example of an inner event (the scarab from the dream) coinciding with an external event (the beetle from the window). Jung said to her, "There's your scarab from your dream."

It's important to note that the scarab was not only meaningful for the patient; it was meaningful for Jung as well, so much so that this example was one he always referred back to when discussing synchronicity.

Most importantly, this wasn't "just a random" synchronicity. The event helped Jung's patient get past whatever was blocking her progress in her therapy, and she was able to move forward after the "beetle incident." Even Jung didn't know the exact mechanism which caused this interesting synchronicity and its effect on the patient's therapy, but he recognized it as significant.

Case Study No. 27: A Confirming Dream

In one of my first dreams of this nature, I found myself in a hotel/conference center that was linked to an airport. I had to get on a plane, but decided to look around the conference first. As I walked in I noticed an older gentleman with some folks around him.

As I got closer, I realized I knew who this was: Mark K., the owner of a company, Edge Research, that had been a direct competitor to my first company, Brainstorm. Mark's company had been bought by Lotus (now part of IBM, but at that time Lotus was one of the largest software companies in the world), over a year before this dream. I hadn't heard from him in all that time, and so I found it odd that he would suddenly show up in my dream after all these months.

In the dream, I was going to ask him why I hadn't heard from or about him in many months, but instead we started with what would be considered a "polite" business conversation. "So how's business?" he asked. I replied and we went on for a little while, making idle chitchat. Then one of us—I can't remember who—said, "I have to go," and we went our separate ways.

I woke up that morning thinking, "How odd! I haven't seen or heard from this guy in at least six months, maybe even a year, and here he is showing up in my dream all of a sudden." Because I hadn't fully developed the idea of "clues in dreams" at this point, I promptly dismissed the dream as a simple oddity, though if I had paid attention to Treasure Hunting Rule No. 1, the oddity itself might have been a marker that this was a clue.

Later that morning, just after I had arrived at the office, I received a phone call from a product manager at Lotus. He was calling to tell me that they (Lotus) were about to release a product that was directly competitive with one of our products. Moreover, it was likely that the market for our own product would dry up after this new product was released by Lotus. I didn't like the sound of this and was a little upset. Before I could flash my anger, a thought crossed my mind.

"How is it," I asked the product manager, "that I've never heard of this product until now?" Lotus was a big company, and it was usually very hard for it to keep any new product a secret for long.

"Oh, it's because it was built by one of our subsidiaries, Edge Research, in New Hampshire. You know them—Mark K.'s old company."

Messing Up Cause and Effect

My dream from that morning suddenly flashed in front of me. I was a little flabbergasted and didn't know what to say. I stumbled through the rest of the conversation quickly. The clue was getting progressively louder.

It was a very clear case of an "inner" event—my dream the night before in which Mark K. suddenly appeared—coinciding with an "outer" event—the phone call about a new product they were releasing the next morning.

The situation had potential serious business implications for our company, so I couldn't dwell on the metaphysical aspects of it for long. I called up my management team and we had to deal with the business issue at hand: that Lotus was putting out a competing product.

It would take our business some time to recover, but it would take me even longer to recover from the *metaphysical* issue raised by this dream—that events in our dreams and events in waking life, confirmed by synchronicity, are not so separate as we might tend to think.

Of course we are all familiar with something from our waking lives appearing in a dream later that same night—but this was the opposite! That something could happen in a dream *first*, and have it point to something that would occur in waking life *afterwards*, was a bit of a shock to my logical view of the world.

This led me to question the nature of time, cause and effect. We'll explore this idea that the future can send information to the past in Chapter 11, "Where Do Clues Come from? A Scientific Perspective," where we will explore the ideas of quantum physics that the past, present and future are not what we think they are.

This experience—of having a dream play itself out in the real world—happened to me again and again, until I could no longer deny the message that something was up.

Searching for Dream Answers: the Symbolic vs. the Literal

While it seemed reasonable to "interpret" purely symbolic dreams in purely psychological terms, this dream was different. Although there were symbolic elements in it (the airport, the conference center), there were also *literal* elements—namely the person, Mark, and his company which had been competitive to ours. The dream involved some *information* about something that actually happened in the business world the next day.

In Western psychology and psychiatry, all dreams are taken to be symbolic. Although Freud pioneered this process of "free association" for modern psychologists, where patients *interpret* the symbols in their dreams, there was nothing new about this approach. For thousands of years, humans have been paying attention to their dream symbols and interpreting them.

One of the most famous Big Dreams in history comes to us from the Bible: the story of Joseph and his brothers. Pharaoh's dream about the seven fat cows and seven lean cows was *interpreted* by Joseph as being about seven years of plenty followed by a severe drought of seven years. By heeding the message of the dream as interpreted by Joseph, Pharaoh was able to save up grain and food during the "fat" years to get his people through the "lean" years.

Unlike in Western approaches to dream analysis, many Native American cultures considered dreams to be important to the living of daily life. Dreams weren't something that you started to pay attention to only when you visited a psychiatrist and had some "disorder" that needed to be cured. Native American tribes, such as the Iroquois, the Ojibwa, the Sioux, the Maricopa, and many others, considered dreams to be of great importance in the lives of everyone in their tribe. Some cultures believed that during the night the soul travels to the "dream world" and brings back information that is important for our "waking selves" to know.

This was often a more literal approach to dreams;

sometimes dreams brought back specific information that had an economic impact on the tribe: where to relocate the camp, where game could be found, etc. In most dreams, you will recognize both *literal* and *symbolic* elements, as was the case in this confirming dream.

What Was This Dream Trying to Tell Me, Really?

Years before this dream of mine, I had read Freud's *Interpretation of Dreams*. I found my old copy and flipped through it. It didn't help much in this context. Because I couldn't seem to get a reasonable, rationalist explanation, I decided to seek answers from spiritual teachers, as I had read that dreams and visions have played a crucial role in the development of almost all religions and spiritual paths.

This led me in a whole different path in my life. I remember, in particular, one conversation I had with a spiritual teacher in Boston.

When I asked her what the dream meant, she replied, rather matter-of-factly: "What you had was a sign."

"A sign?" I asked, incredulously. "What do you mean, a sign? Do you mean a religious sign?" I was more than a little horrified. Here I was, trying to present an image of a serious businessman and engineer, and I was being told I was being given signs.

"It was a sign. A demonstration that was set up for you."

"Set up for me?" I asked, still a bit incredulous, but began to calm down. "Set up by who? And for what purpose?"

"It was a message to you from yourself. It was a demonstration that was meant to show you that you are a dreamer, and if you choose to pursue this path in life, you can make great progress spiritually."

"A dreamer?" I asked again, not sure where this was going, but willing to humor her a bit. "I've been called much worse, you know!"

"A dreamer is someone to whom information comes in dreams and who develops certain abilities in the dream world. This was a sign that you are a dreamer, and that if you pay attention to your dreams, they will reveal a whole new way of life for you."

Down the Rabbit-hole of Dreaming

To be honest, I found this all very interesting, but didn't take it all that seriously. Until, that is, it started to happen again, with people and places who first appeared in my dream state then showing up later in waking life.

These weren't necessarily life-changing Big Dreams— they were often little dreams that dealt with the issues that were boiling up at a given time in my business and personal life, or friends that I hadn't talked to in a while.

Sometimes, I wouldn't even remember the original dream. Rather, I would have the uncanny sense of *déjà vu* when meeting someone the next day who had been in a dream. "Where have I seen this person before?" I would ask, and every now and then, I would remember a dream that had featured either the person now before me in the waking world, or someone from my past who reminded me of this person.

This coincidence of internal events with external events was what led me to find out about synchronicity in the first place, and to the gradual realization that synchronicity is happening all around us.

Toward an Integrated View: Wishes of Our Soul

In the Western literature about dreams, the process usually works the other way. We ponder something in our waking lives, and it makes its way into our dreams.

I would find myself pondering a particular problem during the day, and the next morning I would wake up with the answer. This seemed to be a different phenomenon— sometimes I didn't even recall a specific dream, but the answer to the problem would be there. It could be an answer to a technical problem, or a management problem, or some very personal issue.

As I researched more into dreams, I found what they didn't tell us in physics and chemistry class: that many inventors and scientists found solutions to their problems in dreams—we'll talk more about these guys in Chapter 9, "Problem Solving and Creativity from Dreams: Not Just for Old, Dead People." Two famous examples are August Kekulé, who discovered the structure of benzene and kicked off organic chemistry, and Descartes, who came up with the Cartesian coordinate system, and much of the philosophy of modern science, in a series of dreams.

But the more baffling phenomenon was the one where the cause of the dream happened in the future, not before the dream. In the shamanic traditions, and in many Eastern spiritual traditions, communication with "other worlds" in dreams is not only encouraged, it is a hallmark of being a shaman or healer or spiritual teacher.

Of course, this doesn't mean that we have to become shamans if we want to use our dreams to help us to solve complex physics or business problems. It does mean that whether we are shamans or not, our dreams are calling us to follow the "wishes of our soul." In short, some dreams provide clues to the path we are meant to take in this life.

The dream world provides a way of getting "clues" which, if followed, reveal the unique contributions that we can make to our society as a whole, and by doing so we can bring more *integrity, soul* and *purpose* into the business world. Just as my dream was a sign that I could make a contribution to the business world through dreams, so you too can use your own dreams to find the unique contribution you can make.

My own research and experiences showed me that you don't have to have a Big Dream that is life changing to harness the wisdom that comes in dreams. Many "little" dreams contain valuable insights and energy that can have a significant impact on how we live our daily lives, and usually have much more symbolic information than literal.

Keys to Working with Everyday Dreams

"The most important book you will read about dreams is the one that you write yourself."

–Hugh Lynn Cayce

There are as many approaches to dreamwork as there are cultures around the world. Browse the psychology section of the bookstore and you'll find dozens of books, each claiming to "have the answer" for how to work with your dreams.

Almost all of them agree that writing down your dreams is the first, most important step. Writing down your dreams (or some subset of your dreams) will improve your dream recall and bring the dreaming world closer to the waking world. You can then move on to do dreamwork to try to interpret these dreams.

If writing down your dreams is the first, most important principle of bringing through "dream messages," then the second principle is that only you hold the key to your dreams. In your own personal treasure hunt, the messages and symbols that come through for you in your dreams will be unique to your career path and life path.

This means that the numerous "dream dictionaries" that tell you that dreaming of water is really a dream about "your subconscious mind" may not do much to guide you. In these "dream dictionaries" someone else is telling you *what your dreams mean*, which doesn't often work if you are trying to use your dreams as a guide for you in your own career.

The important thing is that you start to pay attention to your dreams and the symbols and elements that come through them. Each of us is unique, and each of us brings different gifts and inclinations into the world. Why should our dreams be any different?

TREASURE HUNTING RULE NO. 10:

Use the "keys" to unlock the symbols of everyday dreams

In a story I've related elsewhere in this book, a series of "clues" led me to pay attention to the work of Robert Moss, who has written several books on dreaming which combine approaches of Native American (more literal approach) with a Western approach (where dreams are symbolic, psychological functions). Moss later became a mentor of mine and I learned much about dreamwork and shamanic traditions from him.

In his book Conscious Dreaming, Moss gives an excellent set of "keys" to unlocking your dreams. While not exactly a step-by-step approach, these keys can be critical in "opening the letter" that the dream represents. I've shortened the list and added some of my own perspective to these keys to make it easier for your dream symbols to be added to your own Book of Clues.

- **Give the dream a title and a quick description.** The colorful title is an often-recommended technique for improving dream recall. By giving the dream a title, you are giving it a concrete place in your mind and are locking onto the memory of the dream, which can be fleeting and may disappear without some sort of anchor. A descriptive but memorable title is often best. You should typically start your Book of Clues with the date, the title, and a *concise* description of the dream, staying away from any interpretation at this stage of the game. I used to write long descriptions but eventually settled on quick outlines of the elements in the dream, which would make the symbol exploration easier.

- **Pay attention to your *feelings* and the *energy* of a dream.** The way that a dream leaves you *feeling* is an important clue to the nature of the dream. If you dreamed of someone you've just met, and you wake up with an "uneasy" feeling, this is important, and your dream may be warning you to go "slow" and be "wary" of that particular person. Similarly, if you wake up feeling light and giddy and refreshed, then this dream may have been one you needed in order to feel better about things in your life around you.

  Sometimes, the *feelings* that come from or with a dream are the important message. So, if you write down a dream, you should immediately note the feelings associated with it.

  An even more important aspect of how a dream feels is that Big Dreams *feel* different from ordinary dreams. Did the dream leave you with an "uncanny feeling" of some sort? Was it a particularly vivid dream, one that you know you will remember even without having to write it down?

- **Work with the elements of the dream (literal, symbolic).** This is a step that will take you some time, but it can be the most rewarding as it involves interpretation and exploring the dream itself. If you make an outline of the dream and highlight, circle or otherwise identify the key elements, you can quickly figure out if they are literal or symbolic, and start interpreting the symbolic ones.

- **Literal elements.** It is often best to find the literal elements within the dream first, if there are any. As I've said, many dreams contain symbolic as well as literal information. This is why it's important to do what Moss calls a "reality check" on your dreams.

  Are there any elements in your dreams that relate to your "waking life" today or in the past? These could be places you have been which appeared in your dream, people you know, or some aspect of your work or career.

  This is actually the first step in noticing synchronicity in the world around us. By writing down these elements you are "anchoring" them in your mind, so that if they come up later during the day, you'll be able to tie them back mentally to the dream itself.

  Note that the same dream element can be literal at one point in your life, and symbolic at another point. When I was a kid in grade school, at the end of the summer I would often have dreams about the first day of school and the anxiety associated with it. This was a literal element at that point in my life; if I have dreams about school today, it would be considered symbolic because I'm not currently in school.

- **Symbol exploration.** In this phase, you start to analyze the symbolic language of the dream.

  For each key symbolic element in your dream, you should ask yourself, "What does this mean to me?" Write down the first thing that comes to mind. For example, if you notice a spaceship in your dream, you'll want to think about what a spaceship means to you.

Sometimes the meaning of a particular symbol can be the clue that unlocks the whole dream. A friend of mine once had a dream that had "dirty water" coming out of a tap. When she thought about this symbol, the first thing she thought about was the movie, *Erin Brockovich*, where Julia Roberts played a lawyer who stood up (against great odds) to a large corporation that had been polluting the drinking water. By fighting for what was right, she won a great legal victory (and Julia Roberts won the Academy award, too). This one symbol was enough to unlock the message of the dream: to fight for what was right in her own life.

When exploring symbols, pay attention to the people in the dream. A good question to ask yourself about them is "what aspect of myself" do these people represent? While this is a purely symbolic way of looking at the dream, there is usually a reason why a specific person or persons appear in a specific dream. The people in a dream often have both a literal significance and a symbolic significance.

Someone who was a mentor to you in earlier years may appear in your dream to give you advice; you can think of this as a wiser part of yourself. Someone you used to hang out with and go to parties with might be a part of yourself that likes to "cut loose" and not "be so serious."

- **Find the message/bumper sticker.** Once you've explored the elements, you may be able to sum up the dream message. Most dreams have some piece of advice for you. As in the case of the dream with the "dirty water," you usually have to explore the symbols before you find the right message from the dream. This is where interpretation is appropriate. Robert Moss encourages dreamers to come up with a "bumper sticker"— a short pithy phrase that could fit on a bumper sticker that encapsulates the message of the dream. An example of a bumper sticker might be "slow down and learn to appreciate the small things in life," or "don't take things so seriously," or "trees can be fun to climb" or anything you like. The more humorous and memorable the bumper sticker, the more likely the dream is to have an impact on your life.

- **Honor the dream.** One of the most important elements of dreamwork to come to us through Moss from Native cultures is the aspect of "honoring" the dream in some literal way. This means to "bring the energy" of the dream into your life. If a "wise master" were to show up in your life and give you something—a gift, a piece of advice—you'd want to say "thank you," wouldn't you?

   You can honor a dream by doing something physical that reminds you of an aspect of your dream. If you dreamed of a tree, you might want to draw a picture of the tree. Or you might want to buy a plant for your home. If you saw a scene that reminds you of a movie you've seen, you may want to rent that movie. If a person you haven't seen or talked to in a long time appears in your dream, you may want to say hello to that person—send them an email. The key is that by *doing something* related to the dream, you are starting to unblock the channels that exist between the symbolic world of dreams and the literal world around us—you are stretching your "intuitive" muscles. I have found that the more you do this, the more you'll be rewarded. We will explore this idea further for all types of clues in Chapter 7, "Bringing the Clues into the Board Room."

This brings us to the final key, which is what ties the Keys to the Clue Lifecycle and your personal Treasure Map.

TREASURE HUNTING RULE NO. 11:

Validate the dream in the waking world

Looking back at the Clue Lifecycle, if a dream is a clue, then there will be confirmation or repetition of something in the dream. Just as with my dream about a business contact (whose name came up rather unexpectedly the next day), the next day, you can look throughout the day for any elements of the dream that appear in waking life and catch your attention.

Honoring the dream is a good first step in learning to recognize clues that come while we are awake. A great way to do this is based on how you might honor the dream—if you dreamed of someone you haven't seen in a while, you can call or email them. They might tell you something that validates why you had the clue.

A few years ago I had a dream about a friend of mine from MIT who I hadn't seen in a few years. Getting the "funny feeling" that this dream was some kind of a clue, I decided to email her that day to honor the dream. She got back to me that same day and responded: "I've been thinking of calling you—I wrote a business plan and wanted to get your opinion on it, but wasn't sure if it would be an imposition to ask you to read it for me." This provided immediate confirmation that the dream had some tie to the real world.

CASE STUDY NO. 28:

Legally Blonde and the Entrepreneur

Let's run through an example of this process at work with one of my own dreams that deal with career-related issues:

I was arriving at school for "Year 1." It seemed like a financial school, and we were learning about business, securities trading, etc. Somehow I found myself having to attend "Year 1" again. I believe I was allowed to skip it the first time. The first-year students started "teasing" me in the same way that kids might tease an older student who had been held back from advancing to the next grade. They were quite brutal— picking on me—and some of the bullies were actually hitting me.

It wasn't until the first semester of learning about business and finance was well under way that the other students started to see my strengths. They realized that, unlike many of them, I had started a company before and had been through many of the financial scenarios that we were learning about in class. The radical elements got neutralized rather quickly, and soon everyone wanted to work with me and be in the groups that I was in. Someone in the school newspaper did an interview with me, and I became well known around campus.

This was an actual dream I had while I was starting another business. It's an interesting dream to look at because, even though it's relatively short, it shows the many layers of meaning and experience that can weave themselves into a single dream. Let's work through the highlights of the process on this dream:

- **Feelings.** I awoke feeling a little battered, but much stronger and appreciated because of it. This feeling, combined with the subject matter of the dream, which related to business, was a good clue about the meaning of the dream.

- **Literal elements.** Did this dream have any elements that related to or could be recognized in my waking life? I didn't recognize the setting or the people in the dream, so it was very much a symbolic dream. An interview with a newspaper is a literal element that could certainly play itself out at some point in the future. However, I had recently been speaking to some young entrepreneurs, and they all seemed very "cocky" to me. Though the "internet bubble" of the late 1990s had crashed recently, these "young kids" reminded me of the arrogance that I didn't like about the internet boom. This seemed to relate to my dream.

- **Symbol exploration.** One of my first associations when I woke up from this dream was with the movie *Legally Blonde*. This made me laugh, as it was a pretty funny movie. In it, Reese Witherspoon played a character who seemed rather out of place at Harvard Law School. The other students made fun of her way of dressing and her general way of being; however, as the movie went on, she proved herself as a young lawyer and the other students suddenly began to respect her. This paralleled my own dream on many levels.

  As I started to explore the dream, the element of "having to go through the first year" again, after having skipped it, seemed to have a clear meaning in the world of business. It meant having to "go back" and do the "fundamentals" of a business all over again. This symbol was enough to unlock one message from this dream: I was in the process, at the time, of starting my most recent company, related to the new technology called XML, and this seemed to be a message that we would have to build from the ground up, paying attention to the fundamentals.

  If I stuck to this business and followed through with it, I would also get proper respect from the many "first time" entrepreneurs who were just starting out, even though I felt like a student who was forced to redo a grade in school.

- **Message/bumper sticker.** A bumper sticker that came to me when I thought about this dream was, "Your prior experience was valuable, and soon you'll see why." This was an encouraging bumper sticker that could get me through a lot of hardship.

- **Honor the dream.** A good way to honor this kind of dream would be to do something fun and light that still brought through the energy of the dream. Since the dream reminded me of the movie *Legally Blonde*, watching that movie again seemed a perfect way to bring the energy of that dream into waking life. Remember that the lighter and more fun your "honoring the dream" activity is, the more likely you are to carry it out—so don't choose something that's serious and a lot of work.

- **Looking for confirmation/validation.** In the days after this dream, I was approached by some first-time entrepreneurs looking for advice concerning their start-up. This reminded me in general terms of the dream, and I overheard someone talking about "Elle" from *Legally Blonde*. I took both of these as confirmation that the dream had been an important clue for me to keep in mind.

CASE STUDY NO. 29:

The Engineer vs. the Artist

Let's look at another dream, one that required some interpretation but was a Big Dream nevertheless.

Ellen, who was a very creative artist at heart, had been working as a programmer and web designer for corporate clients over a few years. During her job search for her next contract, she had an increasing feeling that this environment was stifling her. Then she had the following dream:

> Ellen had been called (via an agent) for an interview in a very colorless corporate high-rise building. A suit-wearing German woman was to conduct her interview. While waiting to be interviewed, Ellen spontaneously decided to leave the office without doing the interview.
>
> In the following scene, the agent who set up the interview yelled at Ellen on the phone, "You're not playing the game!"
>
> But instead of going back to the company, Ellen found herself in a colorful cobblestoned French-looking area, going to meet her friend Claire. She entered a restaurant that was not yet open, to find Claire, who was wearing a very colorful, flowing dress. Claire was dancing on the tables, whirling around having fun. Ellen spent the rest of the afternoon with Claire, just having fun, in this very colorful part of town.

Ellen worked through the "keys" for this dream, which was to prove very important to her.
- **Title:** "Leaving the Interview for Fun."
- **Feeling.** When she woke up, she had a positive feeling

about the dream, and felt very free and authentic.
- **Literal and symbolic elements.**
  - **Literal:** Ellen often got calls from agents interviewing her for corporate programming jobs.
  - **Symbolic:**
    - The German woman represented being very straight-laced, and left-brained.
    - The agent saying, "You're not playing the game" represented Ellen not being authentic in work situations.
    - Claire: represented her light, artistic self.
    - Colorful, flowing dress and dancing: being free and creative.
    - French: represented more artistic vs. the German.
    - Cobblestone part of town: represented a creative area with character vs. cold, soul-less company environment.
- **Bumper sticker:** "Go with what makes your heart sing!"
- **Honor the dream.** A good, concrete way for Ellen to honor the dream was to take the afternoon off and look into local art courses, which she did.

The confirmation of the dream came as Ellen started to let her inner artist out. She decided to start her own website, "Places of Light," for her spiritual art—www.placesoflight. com, and is now living an artistic rather than corporate life, and is much happier.

EXERCISE

Apply the Keys to Your Own Dreams

Each day for a week, try to work through a small number of these keys for dreams when you first wake up. If you don't have time or the inclination to do the full set of dreamwork, at the very least, write down the title of a dream, and write down any literal or symbolic elements you remember. This is enough to start exercising the muscle of dream recall and for you to start getting a sense of how your dreams work.

As you start to pay attention to your dreams, you'll begin to see the "patterns" that emerge concerning how messages manifest themselves in your particular dreams. I often find myself at school in my dreams; this is a powerful symbol (and reminder) that life and career are a never-ending "process of learning." This is what we call a "recurring symbol"—because it appears in multiple dreams as an ever-present backdrop.

I'm also a big movie-fan, and often find symbols or characters from movies that I've seen appearing in my dreams. At first I thought that this was just about fun; then I realized that what the characters often represented were reflections of what was going on in my own life at the time of the dream.

Try the following keys with your own dreams:
- Give the dream a title and a concise description.
- Pay attention to your **feelings** and the **energy** of a dream.
- Work with the elements (literal, symbolic).

- Find the message/bumper sticker.
- Honor the dream.
- Find validation/confirmation in waking life.

The key to unlocking your dreams is to take the power of them into your own hands. Each of us has different "styles" of dreams; your task is to find your own style, and by paying attention to it, to ease the ability of your conscious mind to receive clues about your life and work. If you do, you'll start to notice that there are very clear indications of the next steps you should take to bring more integrity, soul and purpose into both. You'll start to recognize that clues in the world around you, clues in your own body and clues from your dreams are "conspiring" with you to reveal your unique path unfolding before you.

PART III

THE REAL
WORLD

"Never ignore a gut feeling. But never assume it's enough."

–Robert Heller

CHAPTER 7

Bringing the Clues
into the Board Room

At this point in the book, you may be thinking, well that's all great and interesting, but how do I actually bring the practice of treasure hunting—using synchronicity, dreams and intuition—into the real world, and in particular, into the business world?

After all, most of us have careers that require working with other people and convincing them to go along with us if we have a hunch or clue that we think should be followed.

Surely it's not as straightforward as simply paying attention to your dreams and hunches, and acting on them. Or is it?

This chapter gives some guidelines on how to bring the energy and insights that come with your own personal Book of Clues with you into the modern workplace, and also how to communicate with your co-workers, bosses and subordinates.

From Manual to Automatic

In order to follow the clues of your personal Treasure Map successfully, and use the techniques in this book to bring more integrity, soul and purpose into your work life, you have to start by bringing the hidden worlds (the world of dreams, insights, hunches, imagination) and your ordinary, everyday world closer together.

The process of finding and acting on clues in both the waking and dreaming state is cumulative, just like physical exercise. Exercising once or twice doesn't have the same effect as a prolonged period where you exercise regularly. Similarly, trying it once or twice and then forgetting about it isn't nearly as powerful as building up the *attention* that you're paying to these uncommon sources over a period of time. The more that you learn to follow your clues, the more likely you are to see more clues.

At first, the Clue Lifecycle is a very manual process—writing down the clues, figuring out interpretations, taking action and finding validation. Over time, it becomes much more automatic—you have a funny feeling about entering a particular store or about a particular person and, rather than thinking about it, you learn to just follow it to see where it leads.

Honoring Thy Clues

This brings us to our next Rule of Treasure Hunting:

TREASURE HUNTING RULE NO. 12:

Honor your clues with a concrete action

As we discussed earlier, the mainstream Western approach to dreams is mostly to ignore them and not give them much credence. The mainstream Western psychological approach is to interpret the dream.

However, in many Native American traditions, dreams aren't always meant to be interpreted—sometimes they are just meant to be *experienced*. The process of interpreting dreams—a very mental process—is a very *Western* way of working with dreams. As we've discussed, in many Native American cultures, dreams are viewed more as actual journeys—"flights of the soul"—to specific locales in the dream world, than as something "abstract" and "mental" that needs to be analyzed.

Sometimes, according to many Native American and shamanic traditions, simply experiencing the dream while you are asleep isn't enough. In these traditions, when you have had an important dream, it's important for the dream's energy (which can be just as important as the dream content) to be brought into the waking world. This is a process that has been known to provide healing and energy for individuals and tribes.

As introduced in Chapter 6, "Clues that Come in the Night: Everyday Dreams and Synchronicity," this process is called "honoring your dreams," and it brings your waking life and the world of dreams closer together.

It turns out that this same step can be applied to any clue, not just dreams. You can honor a clue by taking an action in the direction the clue is pointing you, but you can also just do something that will honor the clue even if you are not yet ready to make any changes in your life or work because of it. Once again, the best way to honor the clue is to have a *concrete, physical action* that you perform which is related to your clue.

You might have seen a funny animal in your dream; you can honor it by sketching a picture of the animal. Or your dream might remind you of something you saw in a movie once—you can honor this dream by renting the video and watching it. Or if you see someone in a dream who you know but haven't talked to in a while, send that person an email or call to say hello.

In many Native American societies, healers and chiefs would hear songs and see dances in their dreams.

They would bring these songs and dances into actual ceremonies that played out the energy of the dream. This process honored the dream and frequently resulted in benefits to the person and to the tribe (healing ceremonies, for example) all in one step. It also increased the abilities of the dreamer, because he or she was successful in bringing something from the dream source into the real world.

In following your own clues on your personal Treasure Map, you don't have to do a funny dance or sing a dream song to honor a clue or a dream. But you should find a simple way to *honor* the energy of a clue.

Of course writing it down is the first step, but go a step further. Draw a picture of something that the clue or hunch is reminding you of. Go watch a movie or to the library or bookstore and find something that relates to the clue.

Do a search on the internet and see if you can find an image that reminds you of your clue. Or have lunch with your co-worker who may have appeared in a dream or call your old friend who has a similar name to the bird that you noticed flying around today.

Of course, if you follow the techniques in this book, this may also involve something concrete that *affects* your work. In some business scenarios, this simply means taking some literal action based on the dream. As an example, I had a dream that one of my employees was feeling under-appreciated. I took some time out later that week to spend some time with him and tell him how much we appreciated the work he was doing, and describing some of the opportunities that I saw for him down the road. This not only honored my dream but also potentially prevented a personnel issue that might or might not have come up in the future.

The more you "honor" your clues, the more you'll find that they are *meaningful*. This is because the part of you that reaches out and tells you to notice a particular clue, the "inner mentor," likes to be taken seriously and to be valued, just like any other part of ourselves.

To take the clue seriously doesn't mean you have to be serious—in fact, if the dream had a light quality to it, you shouldn't honor it by doing something serious. Rather, you'll want to honor it by doing something fun and "light." This could involve taking a walk in the park, singing a song in your head, or going to a locale that your clue reminded you of.

CASE STUDY NO. 30:
Honoring the Seashells in Arizona

Let's use a simple example.

A friend of mine from Arizona, let's call her Sue, was telling me about seeing a movie, concerning taking a pilgrimage (the movie was *The Way*, about the Camino de Santiago, a popular walking pilgrimage route in northern Spain). In the movie, she noticed some seashells.

She told me the next day after seeing the film, she had a funny feeling when she was about to drive to work, and decided to look around her driveway. There, off to the side of her driveway, she saw a seashell.

She wondered if this might be a clue. First of all, Arizona is in the middle of the desert in the southwest of the U.S., so she was very far from the coast. The fact that seashells had been on her mind from the movie the previous day reinforced in her mind that this was could be a clue.

The first two criteria (*Was it unusual?* Yes, it was, for Arizona. And, *Did it repeat?* Yes, shells were seen first in the movie, then on the driveway) were both met.

As she looked around, she found another seashell some distance away from her driveway. Now the clue was becoming even more apparent. She was about to get back into her car and drive away when out of the corner of her eye, she saw a third seashell. Now she knew that this was a clue, which is a good first step.

But what was the clue telling her? This was a little more difficult, but she decided to honor the clue by laying out all three seashells in a row and taking a picture. This was a concrete way to honor the clue.

As she wondered about the seashells, she thought more about the movie she had seen the previous day. While she wanted to go on a pilgrimage to the Camino de Santiago, it wasn't exactly practical for her to fly off to Europe on a moment's notice.

She decided that she would take another step in that direction; the seashells reminded her of the film, and the film had to do with a father taking a pilgrimage in honor of his son. She decided that the clue was telling her in the near term to go on a pilgrimage to somewhere closer. She set up a trip to Sedona and took her daughter, who was going through a very rough time. There they both encountered numerous synchronicities that helped her daughter in getting through her current difficulties.

This is a good example of recognizing a complex clue, and taking both an initial step to honor the clue (taking a picture of the seashells), then taking an action based on interpretation of the clue (which was to go on a pilgrimage).

CASE STUDY NO. 31:
Honoring a Dream Leads to a Job

Let's look at another example of how honoring a clue is usually a first step in some larger pattern.

Pam had been thinking about starting a new company or joining a company involved with a new economic model called the sharing economy, but didn't know how to get started. One day, she woke up from an incredibly vivid dream. It was very different from a typical dream. It was somehow more real, more vivid and more memorable.

In the dream she was at a party at her boyfriend's house. A man approached her at the party. He was very clean cut and dressed in a blue polo shirt and khaki pants with a brown belt. Her boyfriend at the time, Richard, was a farmer and usually dressed in jeans and a t-shirt. So this man seemed very out of place at his party.

Pam asked this man, "You aren't one of Richard's friends. Who are you?"

The man in the polo shirt replied, "My name is Yoshito Harvard." (Name changed to protect identity.)

At this point in the dream, Pam saw what could best be described as "data" flying between two different faces on two different computers. Then she woke up.

For some reason, Pam says that she simply knew that the data flying between the two different faces meant that she should look up the name "Yoshito" on LinkedIn. She discovered that one of the early pioneers in the field of study she was interested in, the sharing economy, was a man named Yoshito. She realized this was a clue!

Now, Yoshito's last name in real life was not Harvard. So she wasn't exactly sure how to interpret this, but Yoshito was coming to Boston to speak at MIT just down the road, and she decided to follow the clue and attend his talk. She had no idea why she was going and didn't know what to expect.

At the end of the lecture, she approached Yoshito and asked him if he knew of any technology providers that could help her. He gave her the name of a CEO of a local start-up, let's call him Matt. Pam called Matt and they had a good discussion, but there really wasn't an opening and the discussion seemed to end there.

So at this point, Pam had followed the original clues (from the dream and the synchronicity), and while it had led to an interesting conversation, there was no concrete action to take. This usually happens when you have an interesting clue that is part of a larger pattern, revealed over time.

About a year later, Yoshito's company bought Matt's start-up. The newly acquired start-up was looking for someone to run the new combined product line. Pam sent in her résumé without expecting much, but she got a call back from Matt almost immediately. He had remembered their discussion from the prior year and offered her the job right away.

Pam wasn't sure whether to accept, since it would involve relocating and some personal sacrifice. She also had another job offer in Maine which wouldn't require her to relocate, so she was torn.

She was uncertain whether to follow the clue or not? Synchronistically, she overheard someone say some negative things about the company in Maine she'd been considering. This "overheard" conversation seemed to her another clue, and she decided to accept the new job.

Now, a year after the dream, she works with Yoshito every day. He has no idea about the dream she had and how it led her to this new position.

Sometimes, a series of clues can lead you to a new job or situation. This is a perfect example of how clues are personalized; you may not know where they lead until you follow the clues. Whether you need to tell others about your experience and how you got there is completely up to you, but you should honor your clues!

Communicating with Others

This brings us to our next Rule of Treasure Hunting:

TREASURE HUNTING RULE NO. 13:

Translate your insights into the "language of business"

While you can honor your clues in your own way, one of the most difficult aspects of bringing "clues" that come from dreams and synchronicity into the world of business is the issue of *how best to communicate* these concepts to our fellow inhabitants there. This includes our co-workers, our bosses, our clients, vendors, etc.

I would suggest that there is no one cookie-cutter answer to this problem, as each of us works in a different kind of company and may have to follow slightly different guidelines in bringing these very different worlds and their vocabularies closer together.

One of the best things about technology start-ups, where I have spent most of my career, is that a good idea is often recognized for what it is, regardless of where it came from, or whom it came from. This is not necessarily the case in larger organizations, where the source of the suggestion may overshadow the suggestion itself.

But even in a big organization, where "justification" and "backup" are required before any new idea is pursued, creative problem solving is valued by most executives. In fact, finding a creative solution to a problem that others haven't been able to solve is one of the sure-fire ways to get noticed higher up on the corporate ladder. And many corporations spend tons of money each year to foster so-called "out of the box" thinking. At first glance, the concepts described in this book are about as "out of the box" as you can get when it comes to the corporate world. In order to use the concepts in this book more consciously in the business world, one approach is simply to link them to the vocabulary and language that are *already in use* in the business world.

A friend of mine, let's call her Jill, once presented a product idea to the board of directors of the start-up company she was working for. They seemed to be impressed by the product idea. Then one of the directors asked her, since the idea was pretty far outside the box, "Where did you come up with this idea?" Jill decided to answer truthfully and said, "Serendipity!"

He frowned and started to laugh. Because Jill hadn't used the right language of business, the board member now started to make fun of her rather than take her idea seriously and the idea was quickly forgotten.

In order to communicate successfully, you'll have to learn to share the ideas you receive and the paths you want to explore in terms that can be easily understood by your co-workers. This can be done by translating the language of spiritual insight and clues into the language of business.

Think of this as being no different from translating one language to another—you have to pick the right words, but even more, you have to get the right cultural context, perhaps even the correct idiomatic expressions that are unique to each language.

Not So Different After All

Since most successful businesspersons follow their intuition, this isn't as hard as it may seem at first glance.

Upon closer inspection, you might find that the truth is that successful businessmen and women rely on their intuition *all the time*.

I have been told by start-up investors, for example, that they tend to trust their gut feelings about the entrepreneurs they are investing in more than the business plan or the market strategy. In the business world, when your *feelings* tell you something different from what is being told to you verbally by a business associate, vendor, boss, or even employee, you may want to take that as a "clue" that something is in play that's not in plain sight.

CASE STUDY NO. 32:

A Venture Capitalist Uses Synchronicity to Make an Investment

A venture capitalist in Silicon Valley, let's call him Dan, told me a story once about how he decided to make an investment. He had been pitched an idea that would allow people to use the internet to stream content, including live TV, from their living room to their mobile phones.

This was well before this kind of thing was commonplace with mobile phones. He heard the pitch from the team and liked it, but wasn't sure if he should go ahead and make the investment. He wasn't sure how many people would want to stream their television content to their mobile phones.

That evening, he went to a baseball game. He was sitting

high up in the stands and was far away from the action. In front of him was a father with his son, who seemed to be vision impaired. The son was holding up his phone, and said, just loud enough for Dan to overhear, something like: "It's so hard to see what's going on. I wish I had a little TV on my phone so I could see the players up close."

The important thing here is that when Dan overheard and noticed this specific statement and desire of the kid, he realized that it was a clue related to the company pitch he had heard earlier that day, though he wouldn't have used exactly that language.

Dan decided to invest. Now, it's important that you do not misinterpret this story to say that he decided to invest solely based on a synchronicity. In fact, the synchronicity by itself wasn't the main reason he decided to invest. But it provided the extra edge to a decision he was trying to make about this investment. He still needed to justify the decision to his partners, but he was able to do this and went ahead with the investment.

Using the Language of Business

In the business world, you won't typically hear terms like "dreams" or "synchronicity," but you will hear terms like, "I had a gut *feeling*," "I had an insight," "They made me feel uneasy," or "It was suddenly clear to me that the solution involved X."

I have relied on my intuition heavily throughout my career, and after a while, those around me began to expect that I would come up with new ideas. When I did come up with a new idea, I didn't always let on at first that the idea came from a dream. Rather, I would just say, "I have a feeling that we should look into this."

After some time, others around me have come to rely on my "hunches" and "gut feelings," which allowed me to pay even more attention to inner and outer clues, and be more open about my visions and dreams than I might have otherwise been.

During this process of first masking the sources of my ideas, perhaps being too secretive, and then later possibly being too open about them, I learned to translate the language of "clues" and "dreams" into business terms in my own industry. You too can do this, no matter which industry you are in.

Here are some guidelines to follow, which you'll want to customize for your area of work.

- **Stretch out the effort involved to add credibility.** One important, often implicit belief in the business world (and the academic and political worlds) is "no pain, no gain." While no one will say this out loud, it is true that the credibility of a person, and the length of time they have spent studying something, carries a lot of weight when influencing others. With this way of thinking, someone who simply "dreams the solution" or finds it by "serendipity" isn't always taken seriously—they haven't felt enough pain yet.

  So, instead of saying, "I had a series of synchronicities and a dream last night that led me to this solution," it's probably best to stretch out the effort in describing how you came up with the solution. This could be simply: "I tried the normal approach to solving this problem, but it didn't lead anywhere. I searched and searched and tried several other dead ends. After trying everything else, I finally had a hunch to try this other way." This couches the problem, and your finding a solution to it, in terms that are easily digestible.

- **Use motivation that others will understand when describing your decisions.** You might find that your dreams or clues are calling you in a very different direction from the career or job path that you are currently pursuing.

  If you were to say, "I've been sent a message for the universe that we need to change direction," you will most likely get funny looks (which actually may be OK if you like those sorts of funny looks!). However, another way to couch this message is to use motivations that they will understand: "I've been doing this for a few years and don't find the work challenging any more. I want a fresh challenge and so have decided to do something very different." Or "I'm burned out on this and need some time away." Each of these phrases ("finding your work challenging," being "overworked" or "burned out") uses language and motivations that any of your mainstream co-workers or bosses can relate to.

- **Use similar examples from previous successes to back up your ideas.** "I have an intuition about this" might translate to something like: "You know, this reminds me of the time when such and such a situation occurred. In that situation, the right answer turned out to be something like X, and that's what I think we should look into for this situation as well."

This is a particularly effective and important technique in the world of business. Sometimes, although thinking "out of the box" is given good lip service, most businesses still want to follow a low-risk path to success.

One way to convince others to follow your intuition, guidance or dreams is to link them to some proven business scenario from the past. The ability to do this allows you to show that yours isn't some "wild and crazy idea" that you dreamed up in the middle of the night (which it very well may be!), but really is a culmination of lessons learned from in the past, decreasing the perceived risk.

For example, when I had the dream about a product that looked like a "spider" with XML in the middle, I didn't immediately go out and tell everyone I had a dream about a product with a spider. Rather, I noticed that this type of product reminded me very much of an older product, called DataLink, which had been developed by one of my previous start-ups. That product had been one of our most successful products.

When talking to my co-founders in this new company, I brought up the new product idea by first bringing up the older, successful product. I then drew an analogy between that time and the current time, and about how XML was an up-and-coming new technology that needed linking and conversion tools.

This is a perfect example of using a "scenario" from

the past to provide the right "cultural context" for bringing forth an idea which might have come to you from a dream.

Paying Attention to Clues at Work

Your Book of Clues doesn't just have to be something you have locked away at home in some "altar" or "spiritual corner." Rather, it can be a living, evolving thing. As you pay attention to your dreams, and to the synchronistic world around you, you can start to keep track of "clues" during the day, at work. You might move your Book of Clues from your notebook to your smartphone or tablet, or the other way around.

If you are in a customer-facing job, paying attention to inner and outer clues is a great way to spot market trends, no matter which industry you are in. For example, in my own work, I will sometimes notice when a prospect or customer speaks about a particular technology. If I get a "funny feeling" about one of these, I jot it down in my notebook at work. Later, if someone else mentions this technology, I write it down again, and this starts to become a good way for me to intuit which technology direction my start-up should be taking.

Adding in the Left Brain

Not only does this approach of jotting down clues at work help you to "navigate" in the business world, it also gives you the "backup" that you may need to follow a particular path.

TREASURE HUNTING RULE NO. 14:

Learn to justify your intuition and seek
confirmation

In the business world, you need to add justification for
some new measure before you are likely to get it approved.

One of the best ways to do this is to use your Book of
Clues to create your own business case.

In many of my start-ups, when we meet with potential
and existing customers or business partners, I specifically
keep an eye out for new opportunities based on intuition.
Sometimes we are pitching a customer on X and he says,
"X is nice, but what I really want, what I need tomorrow, is
help with Y." This shows that Y is more urgent for them.
Now, if Y happens to be something we can do with our
existing technology, we need to decide, whether it's worth
pursuing Y. If I find several other customers who also
want Y, then I might have the beginnings of a business
case. The key is to pay attention to your feelings when you
are speaking with vendors, customers, business partners,
etc., and then building up a justification in the language of
business rather than simply blurting out "I have a funny
feeling" about this.

This is how you bridge the gap between the Right
Brain and the Left Brain. The right, more creative side of
the brain is the one that comes up with crazy ideas and
notices clues in the world around you. The left side of the
brain is the skeptic and is typically more analytical.

Finally, as you get more confident in your own abilities,
you'll want to learn not just how to justify your actions,

but also how to influence others in the business world to follow a path that you have seen. This can be done by seeking both backup and confirmation for your clues. We already discussed the "verification" step of the Clue Lifecycle, but this may involve a certain amount of "extra leg work" that can be essential into translating a clue into a coherent path of action that others can buy into without believing in the "woo woo," as the mainstream might call intuition and synchronicity.

CASE STUDY NO. 33:
How Following Intuition Led to the A-Bomb, But Not at First

Let's take a look at how important *translation* is when communicating an insight based on intuition to get the support of others. Specifically, let's look at the insights that led to the atomic bomb. This is a great example where an intuitive vision first had to be translated into one sphere (scientific principle), and then it had to be translated into a whole different world (politics, war) before anyone else could buy into the insight.

When Leo Szilard, a Hungarian physicist, first heard about the splitting of the atom by Otto Hahn and Fritz Strassmann in Germany in 1939, he was concerned that maybe this energy could be harnessed for nefarious purposes. He went to consult Sir Ernest Rutherford, a famous physicist, later dubbed the father of nuclear physics, concerning the possible use of nuclear energy in bombs. But Rutherford was said to have responded:

"The energy produced by the breaking down of the atom is a very poor kind of thing. Anyone who expects a source of power from transformation of these atoms is talking moonshine!"

Leo Szilard was a little discouraged at first. Later, while in London, he had a vision while stepping out into the street as a traffic light changed from red to green. He stopped in his tracks in the middle of the road because of the strength of that vision.

In the vision, he saw not just the splitting of one atom, but that by splitting one atom, it could emit two neutrons, which would go out and impact other atoms, resulting in more fission and more neutrons. If this continued, it would result in a chain reaction that could release unimaginable force. Szilard was intrigued and horrified. His vision was to be a major clue in his life and is one of the reasons that even non-physicists remember Szilard today.

But what to do about it?

He took some *concrete action* on his vision, writing down everything he could think of about how a nuclear chain reaction would work. He didn't think that Ernest Rutherford would be open to his ideas, so he contacted Italian scientist Enrico Fermi and convinced him to work on them instead. He then patented his idea of a neutron-induced chain reaction.

Szilard, a Jew who had fled from Nazi Germany early in the 1930s, was distraught that if this idea occurred to one of Hitler's scientists in Germany, they could develop the atomic bomb first. So he assigned the patent to the British Military so that they could use it to develop an atomic weapon first. But the British didn't seem to understand what they had. There is a great scene in the movie *Day One* where Szilard is handing the diagrams and sketches of his patent over to a British military officer, who responds in a very polite British way, "So that's it, is it?"

Szilard tries to explain that everything is there except for the fissionable material, but it's clear that he's speaking the wrong language. "Very well, jolly good" says the officer giving him a very polite brush-off.

Szilard was a brilliant scientist, but at that point he couldn't find the words to make the military or politics understand the power of what his vision had shown him. Much to his dismay, the British officer put the paper away to be filed in some never-again-to-be-seen place.

It took a few years for Szilard to prove out the concept. He and Fermi both moved to America, and they eventually convinced Szilard's old physics professor, Albert Einstein, to write a letter to President Roosevelt about how the chain reaction could be used to build an atomic bomb.

Even then, that letter sat on Roosevelt's desk for a while, until Einstein convinced a friend of the President, Alexander Sachs, to explain it to Roosevelt. Even after their first conversation, the President still didn't see the potential. In short, it wasn't articulated in language that President Roosevelt understood.

Finally, Sachs decided to join the President for breakfast the next day and told him a story. It concerned a young man, named Fulton, who went to speak to Napoleon concerning a new invention, the steam engine, and how it could be used to power ships. Napoleon thought the idea ridiculous and turned him down. What would have happened, asked Sachs, if Napoleon had shown more vision?

This finally did it. The idea of an "uncontrolled chain reaction initiated by a neutron impacting and splitting the nucleus of the atom" had been translated into language that any politician or general could understand—an unprecedented weapon which would give the Allies a distinct military advantage—an atomic bomb. Roosevelt decided to take action and started funding Szilard and Fermi's experiments, which then went on to become the Manhattan Project.

Though most of us aren't inventing the atom bomb, we may face similar problems when convincing our co-workers to go along with a new idea that we've come up with via our intuition. But by being patient and taking concrete action, eventually translating our idea into the language of our workplace, we too can get projects, great and small, off the drawing board and funded.

How Much Time Does All This Take, Anyway?

A fair question, at this point, might be: how practical is it to pay attention to clues and dreams in the business world? Won't this take up a ton of time?

The answer is that it can take up as little or as much time as you'd like to devote to this process. Clues and "messages" are constantly coming in—the "Stream of Clues"—day to day; it's up to us whether to tap into this stream.

On average, scientists have shown that most people

have up to five dreams a night. Of course, most of us don't remember all of those dreams. Even if you did, writing down five dreams every morning and meditating on them throughout the day, looking for synchronicities, would be enough to make a magical process seem tedious.

The simple answer is to start slow, and to ramp up or ramp down how much attention you're paying to your dreams and synchronicity as it interests you. Remember, the idea of a treasure hunt is that it's supposed to be fun! If you can make your life and career a treasure hunt, you can start to feel magic, mystery and adventure, just like a kid watching an Indiana Jones movie.

It's important to keep this child-like perspective while learning to pay attention to "messages from the hidden worlds." After all, the goal is to live a life that is more fulfilling, and more aligned to the "wishes of our souls."

If you are successful at bringing these techniques into your own life and career, you will start to notice that you are being subtly guided along an invisible set of lines that eventually make up a pattern—a complicated "tapestry" that adds up to the life you were meant to live . . . the real treasure at the end of your personal treasure hunt.

EXERCISE

Bring the Language of Clues into Your Work

This chapter put forward the idea that we can take our clues—our meaningful coincidences, dreams, hunches, uncanny feelings—and bring them into the world of our work and business. I would argue that most successful businesspeople already rely heavily on their intuition, but they know how to translate it into the language of business.

This is a simple exercise, but for those who aren't used to doing so, it requires courage to explicitly bring up clues in your conversations at work. Try doing this at least once a week for three weeks.

Once again, let's start with your Book of Clues. When you have a few uninterrupted minutes, try the following.

1   Pick a clue about work. Look through your Book of Clues to find a dream, synchronicity, funny feeling or hunch that relates to your work.

2   Strategize on how you might talk to others about it. With some people it will be fine to say, "I had a dream about work, and in it . . ." With others, you might say, "I was thinking about this problem and I had a hunch that I'd like to follow up on . . ." You might need to come up with some justification by comparing it to another project or business situation or start-up that was successful, even though that may not have been where your hunch came from.

3   Speak to others in your work about the clue, using the language that is appropriate for your line of work. Notice that in this case you are taking some concrete action and honoring your clue, without knowing exactly where it will lead.

Reflect on how it went. How did the other people react? Did the conversations help lead to some course of action? Did people look at you strangely, as if you had two heads?

Most likely it was something in between, but by learning to talk about your hunches you are starting to bring the world of your personal Treasure Map into the world of your work. The more you do this, the more it will become a habit to "follow" the clues.

"I knew that to do this I had to achieve something much more difficult than anything before. I had to bring my emotions—fear, hope, and greed—under complete control."

–Nicolas Darvas
from *How I Made $2,000,000 in the Stock Market*

CHAPTER 8

Anti-Clues: Patterns and Dragons

A key part of successfully following the clues to uncover your own personal Treasure Map is to become aware of the obstacles that are in your way and learn to deal with them.

In an Indiana Jones-type treasure hunt, the obstacles to finding the treasure might come in the form of Nazis or booby-traps. In our own personal treasure hunt, the obstacles may not be so obvious; they are usually much more subtle and often come in the form of our own patterns and tendencies.

How can you overcome obstacles on the path if you don't recognize them? The key is to learn to recognize "anti-clues," which are clues that can make you aware of your own patterns. Before we delve into anti-clues too much, let's talk a little about patterns.

Learning to follow your own clues goes hand in hand with learning to recognize your own patterns. Just as a GPS system needs multiple satellites to get an accurate reading, so your own inner GPS often needs multiple reference points before deciding what an accurate course of action is.

A comprehensive guidance system utilizes both the left and right sides of the brain. Too often, we are told to "follow our intuition" and find ourselves in a situation that we can't get out of. On the other hand, if we can learn to recognize the inner clues that lead to our external patterns, we will not only get better at following our clues, but we will also get better at understanding ourselves and overcoming our patterns.

External Patterns Repeat Themselves

What is a pattern? I remember meeting a fairly successful businessman who told me near the beginning of my career that if something happens three times, then there's a pattern. His point was that if something happens once, it may or may not be a fluke. If it happens twice, then it's possibly a pattern. If it happens three times, then it's almost definitely a pattern.

Freud once said that the danger of self-analysis is that we are too soon satisfied with an incomplete explanation. The same is true when dealing with our internal and external patterns, because understanding them relies on analyzing ourselves.

Introspection is difficult because we are inside the bubble of our life and our perception is limited. Because of this, in order to recognize our patterns, it's best to start by looking at our "external patterns"—this is a much more objective way to identify what's happening inside each of us as we make major decisions. Once we've done that, we can start to delve into the inner patterns that drive us.

An external pattern is a result in the external world that has been repeated more than once in your career or personal life.

Let's take two examples of external patterns that are very illustrative:

CASE STUDY NO. 34:

Getting into Business Relationships You Can't Get Out of

I was on a radio show once and a woman—let's call her

Lisa—called in and told me that she had a pattern where she would get into business relationships that she no longer wanted to be in, but she couldn't easily get out of them.

"Has it happened at least three times?" I asked, and she answered that it had. "Well then, you have successfully identified an external pattern." She wanted some help in unwinding this pattern so that she could be more successful.

When I asked her how this happened, she said that when she met people they seemed to have good proposals and she got excited at the prospect of working with them. But once she started working with them, she often realized that she wanted to get out of the relationship because it wasn't proceeding in the way she expected.

We'll explore my advice to her about overcoming this pattern soon, but it's important here that she recognized this "external pattern." It's a necessary first step.

CASE STUDY NO. 35:
The Entrepreneur and the Advisor

I worked with an entrepreneur once—let's call him Nigel—who had a pattern related to advisors and investors. He would recruit a new advisor or investor and be very excited about working with this person. He would brag about the new advisor to his other advisors/investors (myself included) and would start to consult with them on all major decisions.

He'd follow the advice of this new advisor, to the exclusion of advice from others, always prefacing it with,

"Well, X says I should do Y, and he is really experienced." Inevitably, one or more of these decisions would not go well. Then he would get upset with the advisor and start bad-mouthing him to the rest of his investors, saying, "X made me do Y, and it was a bad decision."

The first time this happened, I didn't think anything of it. But then it happened with another investor, and then the pattern repeated with an employee. Nigel would never take any responsibility for his own decisions, and always said it was "because of X, I did Y." He could fire the employee, or disassociate from the advisor, but he couldn't recognize that his own actions, his own internal motives were the true cause of this external pattern.

Then I realized he was doing the same thing with me! When it was convenient, he would listen to my advice, and then at some point change his mind and start bad-mouthing me to his other investors/advisors. There was clearly a pattern, but it was one that he was completely unaware of. Paralleling the old saying about history, those who are unaware of their patterns are condemned to repeat them again and again.

Patterns are Like Dragons

These are, of course, negative patterns we've been discussing thus far, and they can seriously get in the way of our being successful in our careers and personal lives. Moreover, they can distract us from the "real work" we are here to do.

But unlike the unredeemable cartoon Nazis in the Indiana Jones films, our negative patterns aren't all bad.

In fact, each negative pattern is usually set in motion by some positive aspect of ourselves—a *strength*.

The fact that Lisa got into such business relationships quickly was a reflection of her enthusiasm for jumping in and wanting to "get going" on projects. The reason that Nigel had his advisor/employee problem was that he was pretty good at recruiting talented individual advisors and employees to his company, and very good at seeking and taking advice.

As I thought about my own patterns and those of other entrepreneurs I've met, I realized that patterns are like dragons. There's an old Chinese saying about dragons:

> If you try to fight the dragon, it will defeat you.
> If you try to feed the dragon, it will eat you.
> But, if you learn to ride the dragon, only then can
> you take advantage of its might and power.

The key to overcoming our patterns is not to fight them, but to learn to ride them, because almost all of our patterns are born out of aspects of ourselves that reflect our strengths. However, by not recognizing our patterns, we often end up finding a way to turn our strengths into weaknesses.

Years after I first heard this expression I was in China and went on a tour of an old temple in Shanghai that had dragons over the doors. The tour guide pointed out something that I hadn't noticed in the dragons initially; each of them was guarding a "pearl" under its claws. Traditionally, the tour guide said, dragons wanted to protect their pearl and they fought each other for them.

This gave another powerful metaphor. If our patterns are like dragons, then each of them is hiding a pearl, a pearl of wisdom in this case, which can help us to become more successful.

This brings us to our next Rule of Treasure Hunting:

TREASURE HUNTING RULE NO. 15:

To see external patterns, pay attention to internal clues

So how do you recognize external patterns? The key is to reflect and learn to recognize that there are clues that indicate we are going down the path of repeating a specific pattern. These clues range from similar situations ("external clues") to bodily sensations ("internal clues") that occur as we make decisions that lead us down a path that ends up repeating our patterns.

First of all, most people who start following their intuition tend to be either those who jump in quickly by being "too trusting," or those who "don't act quickly enough when opportunity calls."

In my book, *Zen Entrepreneurship*, I described a pattern of mine that had happened many times in my life. I would start off really excited about a project, would jump in and immerse myself in it, and then would find something else interesting and jump in and immerse myself in that too. Eventually, the work on projects started to suffer because I had too many projects going on, and I had lost interest in the first ones.

Now, each of these projects individually called to me, so I jumped in. You might even say that I was "following the clues" of my intuition, much like I've been advocating in this book, to uncover my own personal Treasure Map.

I was a bit impulsive in this way, but knowing this and recognizing the pattern is the key to bringing both sides of the brain together to formulate a response.

In my case, there is a "rush" that comes from jumping into a new project, whether it's personal or professional. I like to create things—products, books, companies, video games, films, and I can feel that pull when a new project calls to me. I immediately start to visualize what the final product will look like and the satisfaction I will get from it.

This isn't something I do consciously—it all happens unconsciously, and then I end up "committing" to or jumping into a new project.

Learning to Ride the Dragon

So, when should a clue be followed and when is it an "anti-clue"—a clue that is testing your pattern?

This is where internal sensations ("inner clues") can be very helpful, and it brings us to our next Rule of Treasure Hunting:

TREASURE HUNTING RULE NO. 16:

Learn to ride your dragon by leveraging the
Clue Lifecycle

The Clue Lifecycle was formulated so that you can find clues and follow a process before "jumping in" fully. This process was *meant* to provide a way for you to accumulate clues and to pay attention to funny feelings and internal sensations that come with external events before jumping in.

The first stage of the Clue Lifecycle is *intuition*—this is when you notice something odd is at play, in the form of a funny feeling, a feeling of *déjà vu*, a synchronicity, or some other sensation that is invoked by an external event.

The second stage, *interpretation*, is to figure out what the clue is telling you. But often, it may not be clear exactly what it's telling you—it may be a clue that's encouraging you to go ahead, or an "anti-clue" that's tempting you to repeat an undesirable pattern.

Now, someone with my particular patterns might jump right from "intuition" to "action"—skipping "interpretation" and "confirmation." But, "confirmation" is the key to both uncovering your own personal Treasure Map and uncovering anti-clues.

By waiting for "confirmation" you are asking the universe (or your guides, or the quantum foam, or your angels or wherever clues come from) for more clues to make it clear to you which direction to go in.

In my own case, because of my pattern of jumping in, I need to slow down and consider the clues before proceeding. Once I recognized that I was at the intuition stage, rather than jumping right to the action stage, I have been able to set up a strategy that says, "OK, I've got one clue. Let me wait until I get confirmation before taking any action."

Instead of taking a full action, another strategy that I use is to take a half-step. A "half-step" would be something along the road that the clue is pointing to, but it requires further confirmation.

A half-step allows you to set conditions before proceeding too far. So I might say, "I have a clue that is telling me to quit my job but I don't know if I should." A half-step would be not to quit the job but to set a condition or a timeframe, "I am going to start looking for other jobs or talking to my friends, but I will not make a final decision yet."

By taking a small action, you can wait for further clues— in the form of "validation" that you did the right thing.

For someone who is more cautious than me, who is unlikely to jump at the first sight of a clue, confirmation allows them to proceed with more confidence. It brings in conditions that can satisfy the Left Brain and help them to proceed with confidence.

CASE STUDY NO. 36:
Going from East to West in Mountain View

As another example, I recently bought a house in Mountain View, California, where I currently live and where I have started several companies. Not only is

Mountain View the home of Google, it is also considered the birthplace of Silicon Valley, since Fairchild Semiconductor, one of the very first silicon companies, was based there.

I'd wanted a house within walking distance of the downtown area, which has many bookstores and restaurants. It took several years of looking but I finally found a house that would fit and bought it. I was now within walking distance of my latest video-game start-up, Midverse Studios, so I could walk to work. More importantly, I could walk to my favorite restaurants and bookstores.

However, as soon as I moved in, I found myself in the process of selling my start-up to another company. This was a good thing, because the start-up wasn't going all that well, but after just having moved, partly to be able to walk to work, I would no longer have an office there. Also, one of the bookstores that I loved in Mountain View (a used bookstore called BookBuyers) had hit financial troubles and moved out of the area. I had wished I could help save that store, but I was too busy with my start-up at the time.

Literally two weeks after I'd moved to downtown Mountain View, I heard that my favorite New Age bookstore, East–West, which is the largest metaphysical bookstore in Northern California, located in the heart of downtown Mountain View, was for sale.

I got a whoosh of sensation. I was now living within walking distance of this store, and was in a financial position to buy it. I'd long wanted to own a bookstore, and had been thinking about creating metaphysical apps and perhaps even starting a publishing company.

Was it a dream come true? Was it a series of clues repeating themselves?

The clues were ringing loud and clear. I had also recently become acquainted with Watkins—the oldest metaphysical bookstore in London, which had been purchased by a tech entrepreneur. He then subsequently purchased Watkins Publishing. When I heard this story of the tech entrepreneur who had purchased a bookstore and then later a publishing company, I had a strange set of sensations. I couldn't understand why I was so fascinated by the story, except possibly that I was catching an echo of something in the future.

On the other hand, I worried that I was hyping up the clue too much and that, possibly, it was fitting into my old pattern. Was it an anti-clue? The thing I really wanted to do was to start publishing metaphysical apps and working with authors. Would owning a bookstore actually distract from that, with all of the day-to-day responsibilities?

Rather than jump in, I took a deep breath and considered my old pattern. I had just sold my last company, and one thing I know about myself is that I am not the kind of guy who can go into a role like the manager of a bookstore and deal with all the day-to-day things— within a few months I knew I'd want to go off and start something else.

So, what to do? I took a half-step, and set some conditions. If I could get comfortable with the financial issues and find someone who I had confidence in to manage the store day to day, while I focused on higher-level strategy and the digital enterprise, then I would think about moving ahead. If not, then I would thank the clue for showing me my pattern—it would become an anti-clue.

It's important to follow the full Clue Lifecycle and set conditions on the universe before making major life-changing decisions like buying a business or moving jobs.

Internal Patterns Start in Our Bodies

In this example, I was ready to jump ahead—I could feel the rush and excitement of a new project. By recognizing these internal sensations, I was able to pull back and say, "OK, the intuitive side of the brain is picking up clues here strongly, but let me use my own personal clue strategy—the half-step—to bring the right, logical side of the brain into play so that I can make a decision that respects both."

I needed time and confirmation and validation to figure out if this was an "anti-clue," in which case in a few months I would want to move on and would regret jumping in. This brings us to our next Rule of Treasure Hunting:

TREASURE HUNTING RULE NO. 17:

Take a deep breath and recognize internal clues

So, let's go back to the example of Lisa, who kept getting into business relationships that she couldn't get out of. I suggested to her that there was probably an initial excitement and "rush" when she was discussing a business relationship. If she recognized that excitement, then it was an "inner clue" that she should pay attention to.

I told her that rather than jump in, she needed to pull back and take a few deep breaths, both figuratively and literally.

If our external patterns are caused by our inner patterns, then where do these patterns live? They live in our bodies, our thoughts and our memories. In short, they are part of our "energetic field"—more specifically, the pattern is actually how we hold our energetic field.

Because our patterns live in our bodies and our energy fields, before you make any important decision, you need to take a deep breath. Not just one, but *several* deep breaths. Better yet, do some Yoga and meditate over a few days. This not only gives us the chance to get a better perspective, but also literally unwinds the way we are holding our energy so that our habitual patterns affect us less.

What the Yogis Say: Khosas and Samskaras

According to ancient Yogic texts, our energy fields consist of a series of clear sheaths, or *khosas*. These sheaths normally let light in and out—which means that you can see clearly what's happening around you and how you are affecting it. As we go through life, we create imperfections, or *samskaras* in these sheaths, and we can no longer see clearly.

Yoga and meditation both have a literal physical effect on these imperfections; they iron them out, at least temporarily, until we are able to transform.

Where do these samskaras comes from? According to the Yogic texts, our habitual, repetitive thoughts and desires ("*vrittis*") as we go through life that get lodged in our bodies and energy fields and make an impression on them. In this sense, we are literally bending ourselves (or at least our energetic fields) out of shape as we go through life. And that's how we're making decisions: with a field that is distorted in a particular pattern, a pattern that is unique to each of us!

I actually found that Yoga helped me to clear my mind, which helped me to deal with my patterns, long before I'd learned about the terms *samskaras*, *khosas* and *vrittis*. As I started to reflect on external and internal patterns, I found that there was a Yogic term for our tendencies caused by the *samskaras* in our field: "*vasanas*." *Vasanas* are actually behavioral tendencies which are not only caused by impressions in our field (*samskaras*), but also cause us to have the same thoughts and desires (*vrittis*), that lead us to repeating our mistakes.

So, take a deep breath. Do some Yoga or exercise. Before you jump in fully, give yourself and the universe half-steps that you can take, and let the Clue Lifecycle play out. You will find that you have suddenly become much better at discerning which parts of your Treasure Map are genuinely calling to you, and which are obstacles placed in your path.

Patterns, Clues and Anti-clues on the Treasure Hunt

Every adventure has obstacles—whether it's Indiana Jones searching for the Holy Grail, Luke Skywalker rescuing a princess from the Death Star, or Frodo trying to destroy the Ring. The hero always has to overcome significant obstacles *before* finding the treasure.

In the great adventure stories, these obstacles are external and easily identifiable—the Nazis, Darth Vader, Gollum or the evil wizard Saruman. But as each of us goes through our own adventure in this life, trying to find the work we are meant to do and the people who are meant to help us, recognizing these obstacles is not always as easy.

Just like these heroes, however, we have to overcome obstacles. Ours are subtler, they come in the form of our internal and external patterns, and only by becoming clear-sighted can we succeed. Every adventure has false clues, or anti-clues, which can take us off the right path. These are our own patterns, our inner dragons.

This leads to the conclusion that the real adventure is internal, whether you are trying to destroy the ring in Mordor, or build a life for yourself as a published author or successful entrepreneur, or just find a job that you are happy at.

The last chapter of *The Lord of the Rings* actually takes place when the hobbits, who have been on this incredibly epic journey to help defeat the Dark Lord, find themselves back in the Shire, the home they left at the start. The import of this last chapter is to show how the adventurers have changed internally and reintegrated into their home. That is, in the end, the most important adventure of all.

EXERCISE

Learning to Recognize Your Patterns and Anti-clues

This chapter put forward the idea that sometimes we see clues and are tempted to follow them, but we shouldn't. These are "anti-clues" and they are a perfect way for us to understand our external and internal patterns.

Let's start by examining our external patterns, particularly those that lead to "negative outcomes."

1   Find a situation that didn't turn out as well as you had hoped. This should be an external result (a "negative outcome"). It doesn't always have to be at work; it could be in some other part of your life.

2   Now ask yourself: were there other times when this same type of situation, or a similar "negative outcome," happened in your life?

   a.   If the negative outcome was that you started a project really excited but ended up disillusioned, did this happen on multiple projects?

   b.   If the negative outcome had to do with trusting another person (a business partner, advisor, employee) and finding out that they weren't quite as competent as you originally thought, has this happened with multiple people?

   c.   If the negative outcome happened because you put yourself into a situation you weren't equipped to deal with, did it happen multiple times but in completely different situations?

3   Write down the times that this has happened, and if you are able to find three times, then you are on to something—you have found an external pattern.

4   Examine the decisions that led up to this pattern, each time. Try to remember the steps that led to this internal pattern.
    a.   Ask yourself, what emotion or sensations led to making those decisions? Was it excitement? Was it "being caught up"? This is usually a positive emotion.
    b.   Identify the symptoms—the bodily sensations that accompany this emotion—that are your "inner clue."

Now that you have identified an internal "anti-clue," the next time you find an "external" clue to follow, you have to ask yourself: is it accompanied by its own "anti-clue"? The key when you see the anti-clue and a pattern that might be repeating itself is to follow the full Clue Lifecycle and come up with half-steps you can take before you proceed. You may still end up following the clue, but only after you have gone through a self-correction for your patterns.

"[While dreaming], we draw on a power of invention which it would puzzle us to equal with our eyes open."

–Frederick Greenwood
editor of the *Pall Mall Gazette* [1]

CHAPTER 9

Problem Solving and Creativity from Dreams: Not Just for Old, Dead People

Thus far it may seem that clues are coming to you from the universe or from your unconscious, unbidden to guide you during your life. While this is often how clues come, in this chapter I want to emphasize that they can be used consciously to help us solve difficult problems in our life and work.

This is particularly true of clues that come in the night—in our dreams. Although this chapter will focus on how to draw upon the power of our dreams, the same process can be applied to waking clues. You can "ask for" an answer in your dreams or you can "ask for" synchronicity to show you the answer in the world around you.

Problem Solving while Asleep

The experience of dreaming is a universal tool for problem solving—and happens to all humans across cultures and professions. The Islamic practice of *Istikhara*, which is a formal or ritualized way of asking God for guidance, is still commonplace today. Originally it was a way to ask for a sign in a dream; the person asking for guidance would wait over three days, examining their dreams closely for an answer or a sign.

The examples given in this chapter are typically dreams or visions that came after being "asked for" by the dreamer. However, it's important to note that in the examples given here, the dreamer may not have *explicitly* asked for an answer. But, simply by stewing on some problem for a period of time, they were *implicitly* asking for a solution.

I want to emphasize one point: the use of clues (waking or dreaming) for problem solving and making major life decisions is not something that existed *only in ancient times*, but goes on to this very day. We can use our dreams and the insights that come to us in clues as a powerful source for problem solving, creativity and inspiration. This chapter is about how to ask for a solution to a particular problem or issue in your career or life.

Let's start with a few examples of how dreams have affected the worlds of art, culture, politics, science and technology, and see if we can learn anything from them.

Dreams and the Arts: Some Examples

Dreams can be an incredible source of creativity and new ideas for writers, storytellers, even painters and musicians. Many a creative person has seen or heard an incredible composition in their dreams and then, in an attempt to reproduce what they've seen in their dreams, has created enduring works of art.

Here are a few examples.

- Luis Buñuel, a famous film director from the early twentieth century, made his first film, *An Andalusian Dog,* from his dreams.[2]
- Salvador Dali used imagery from his dreams extensively in his paintings, including his famous image in *The Persistence of Memory* of clocks drooping, which came to him after reading *The Interpretation of Dreams* by Freud.[3]
- Robert Louis Stevenson came up with the plot for *The Strange Case of Dr. Jekyll and Mr. Hyde* while he was

dreaming. After waking up from a particularly frightful dream, he wrote the entire book in three days.

- The famous film directors Ingmar Bergman and Orson Welles both used imagery from their dreams in their movies. They typically shot some of the scenes in their movies as attempts to reproduce what they had seen in their dreams.

- Giuseppe Tartini, an eighteenth-century violinist, had a dream in which he heard the devil playing a tune. Tartini was so enchanted by what he heard that he tried to reproduce as much as he could remember. The result was his most famous composition, "Devil's Trill."

- In Chapter 1, we studied the story of a young James Cameron and his idea for *The Terminator*, which came from a dream of robots emerging from an apocalyptic fire.

- The Beatles tell the story of how the melody for the song "Yesterday" came to Paul McCartney in a dream. The next day he asked his band-mates what song had a melody like the one he'd heard in the dream, which he hummed to them. When they couldn't find any existing song with that melody, he came up with the words for the now famous song.

Dreams and Politics: Some Examples

You might be thinking, "OK, that's fine for creative types, but can dreams really help in more practical professions?"

How about politics? I have already mentioned the role that Deganawidah's dream of a "Tree of Peace" played in the establishment of the League of the Iroquois. He was solving a problem related to the issue of how to deal with his neighboring tribes, who were always fighting against and otherwise undermining each other. The success of the structure of the Iroquois Confederacy had a direct impact on the formation of the Constitution of the United States of America, which in turn influenced many other governments around the world.

But this is not the only, nor even the most influential example of how dreams have impacted on politics and the world order. In history, there are numerous examples, ranging from Genghis Khan's dreams of conquest, Muhammad's dream of the angel Gabriel, to Constantine's conversion to Christianity after having a waking vision.

It might surprise you to learn that this process continues into modern history. Here are several examples from more recent centuries:

- Mahatma Gandhi, during the 1940s, was frustrated when violent protests broke out all across India. He tried making speeches and writing letters, but was rebuffed. Unsure what to do, he finally decided to go into retreat and fasted and prayed for several days. Then one morning he awoke from what he calls "a compelling dream" and immediately called Nehru and others to start implementing his "dream vision." This is definitely what we would call a "Big Dream." He dreamed that he should call together all of the religious parties in India and urge a specific type of civil unrest—*hartal*—an ancient Sanskrit word meaning a day of prayer and fasting. This was the inspiration for the peaceful civil disobedience that contributed greatly to securing the independence of India and Pakistan from the British.[4]

- General George S. Patton often came up with battle strategies in the middle of the night—initiated by his dreams. His personal secretary, Joe Rosevich, was used to getting calls from Patton at all hours of the morning to dictate the next day's battle strategies.[5]

- As we saw earlier, Lyndon Johnson had an important dream that resolved his dilemma of whether to run for re-election or not in 1968. His dream involved being caught in the water between two shores—which he interpreted as the war in Vietnam and his great social programs—and not being able to swim successfully to either shore. After this dream, Johnson later wrote, he made his decision not to run and slept "like a baby" for the rest of the night.

Dreams and Science: Some Examples

Dreams have played a particularly important role in the development of almost all fields of modern science, and as a result have impacted on many areas of technology and industrialization.

- The famous Russian chemist, Dmitri Mendeleev, spent a lot of time looking for an "organizing principle" for the different elements that he was studying. They seemed to occur at random and he could not find any way to organize them coherently. Then, one day, while he was taking a vacation on the Black Sea, he decided to excuse himself from the chamber music that was habitually played in his summer home during the afternoon and took a nap. While napping, and being barely conscious of the music next door, he saw in a dream the elements arranging themselves in a beautiful pattern, not unlike "repeating scales of music." When he awoke, he was extremely excited and immediately sketched out his first draft of the "periodic table" that is still in use today.[6]

- Neils Bohr, another famous physicist, also struggled with figuring out the basic principles of the physical world. He was trying to understand why elements arranged themselves as they did in the periodic table, and why there weren't elements in between the ones listed. One day, Bohr had a dream that he was visiting a racetrack. He noticed that the lanes of this track— which the horses were supposed to stay within—were divided by very thick chalked lines. The horses could "switch lanes," but only if they "were sufficiently separated not to bump." Any horse that was found "outside a lane" was immediately disqualified. When he awoke, he realized that he had discovered the answer to his questions about "discrete elements." This led directly to the formation of his Nobel Prize-winning theories about "electrons" going around the nucleus in "pre-defined" orbits; they could only switch orbits if they had sufficient "energy."[7]

- As we saw earlier, Elias Howe invented the sewing machine when he saw the solution to the critical technical problem of how to thread the needle in a dream. In his dream, he was trapped by cannibals holding long spears that had holes at the pointy end, which gave him the idea of putting the hole at the tip of the needle.

- Frederick Kekulé, a German scientist who made great contributions to Organic Chemistry, was stumped as to the structure of the benzene atom. He tells in his own words in 1865 how a dream revealed the ring-like structure to him:

> There I sat and wrote my Lehrbuch, but it did not proceed well, my mind was elsewhere. I turned the chair to the fireplace and fell half asleep. Again the atoms gamboled before my eyes. Smaller groups this time kept modestly to the background. My mind's eyes, trained by visions of a similar kind, now distinguished larger formations of various shapes. Long rows, in many ways more densely joined; everything in movement, winding and turning like snakes. And look, what was that? One snake grabbed its own tail, and mockingly the shape whirled before my eyes. As if struck by lightning I awoke. This time again I spent the rest of the night working out the consequences.[8]

Not Just for Old, Dead People

These are but a few examples of how dreams have influenced us right into modern society today. Inherent in all these examples is what I like to think of as "bringing together" the dream world and waking world. In each case, the dreamer had some situation in the waking/physical world that was weighing on him—a story, painting, political situation or scientific problem. The dreamer struggled to find answers in waking life. In most cases, the dream brought together, in either symbolic or literal form, the key to answering the outstanding issue. And most importantly, in each case recorded here, the dreamer *acted on his dream.*

Once again, I pose the question that if artists, writers, scientists and even political leaders can use their dreams as an uncommon source of ideas and creativity for furthering their careers, then why not ordinary businessmen and women? Why not accountants and engineers, salespersons and CEOs?

There is no reason why this creative facility, which is available to us all, should not to be used in this fashion. In fact, many successful businessmen and women do precisely this without even knowing they are doing so, because memory of their dreams fades into unconsciousness within moments of waking up.

Ask and Ye Shall Receive

This process of bringing a problem you might have in the waking world and asking for a solution is often referred to as "incubating" a dream. The first step in "incubating" a dream is to "ask for the solution" to a problem, either explicitly or implicitly.

This can be a formal process—a ritual way of asking for a dream by writing down the question or praying for a solution. Or it may be done completely informally by giving the problem our mental attention during the day, as in the examples of the scientists who were struggling with a technical problem for many days before the answer came to them in a dream or vision. This brings us to our next Rule of Treasure Hunting:

TREASURE HUNTING RULE NO. 18:

Ask for a solution in your own way

Gandhi asked for his dream in a ritualized way, including going on a retreat and fasting and praying for several days. This is not unlike the Native American process of going on a "vision quest"; the dreamer goes out in nature, alone, and fasts for a period of time, asking the spirits for a vision.

However, incubating a dream or asking for a solution to a given problem doesn't have to be a formal or conscious process, nor is it done in *exactly the same way for each person.*

In fact, the scientists and inventors Mendeleev, Bohr, Howe, Kekulé and others incubated the dream simply by thinking about their scientific problems all day long. This resulted in an "incubation period" where their unconscious was engaged in helping to solve the problem. Because they spent day after day thinking about the problem, they were asking their unconscious about it, and by trying to visualize a solution they were engaging the part of their mind through which we remember dream images.

In *Conscious Dreaming*, Moss tells of the ancient Greek temple at Asklepios, the Greek god of healing, where individuals would gather from many miles around in order to ask for a healing dream. They would bring gifts—including wheat cakes and honey—and "camp out under the stars," hoping to receive a dream of healing from Asklepios.

Today, you don't have to become a pilgrim to a Greek temple, or leave your tribe to go on a "vision quest," in order to incubate a dream effectively. Each of these was a culturally acceptable way to "ask for help" from the world beyond the conscious mind.

Though we don't need such elaborate mechanisms today, we can still ask for the solution in a way that will engage our dream source. A simple way to do this is to write down the problem you are trying to solve just before you go to sleep.

You can add this to your "ritual of the moon"—which is whatever you do just before you retire for the night. In addition to brushing your teeth, or the other steps you take, you may want to add one more: to ask for the solution to your problem.

The Incubation Period: Letting Go

For some people, asking once in a formalized way is enough to incubate a dream. For others, like myself, it usually requires repeating the request for guidance several times throughout the day. By bringing my attention to a particular problem at several points each day, I find that I am "priming" the pump for a dream to present the solution at some point in the future.

Asking for a solution once, or even several times in the same day, may not by itself be enough. The word "incubation" is a good one because it implies that not only do you need to "bury the egg"; you may also need to "sit on it" for some time. This might mean, after you have "asked for a solution" one or more times, that you need to forget about it for a bit.

In the book *Higher Creativity: Liberating the Unconscious for Breakthrough Insights*, Willis Harman and Howard Rheingold define this process more formally by examining the process of getting creative insights.

The first stage is referred to as the *preparation* phase, where you are actively asking for a solution to your problem. They call the second phase the *processing* phase, when you actually forget about the problem and let it process through your unconscious. I would refer to this as "incubation."

The process of "letting go" is an important one, because it removes your conscious mind from the equation and lets a truly creative solution emerge. This phase also involves a certain amount of relaxation. Mendeleev was in a relaxed state at his summer home when he had the dream about the periodic elements, Gandhi's fasting and meditating played an important role in calling forth his dream, and Kekulé had fallen asleep in front of the fireplace when he saw his vision of the snake eating its tail.

We are all aware of the story of the Greek engineer, Archimedes, receiving his insight while he was in the bathtub, and then yelling "Eureka!" and running out naked into the streets of Ancient Greece.

Leo Szilard, who came up with the idea for the fission-based atomic bomb, was infamous for sitting in his bathtub while doing "work"; it relaxed him enough to let his mind wander free.

This is a perfect example of the type of relaxation that often leads to the solution to a particular problem. The solution may come in a dream, when you are asleep and your conscious mind is turned off, or it may come while you are in a daydream or other form of reverie while relaxed, like Archimedes. To use the language of this book, it may come in the form of a clue that you notice inside a dream, or a clue that you notice in waking life, or during the in-between state when you are falling asleep or waking up.

Illumination: When Inspiration Strikes!

The third phase identified by Rheingold and Harman is *illumination*, when you are presented with a solution. The moment when you "awaken" from the dream, reverie or vision that brings the solution to your problem is an important one.

In some cases, as in the case of Elias Howe, the moment he awoke he realized he had solved his problem of how to thread the needle for his sewing machine. In other cases, you may *know* that you found the solution to a problem, but may since have forgotten it! This means that you'll have to go into the same dream experience again to find the solution!

It's important to write down the dream that you think contains the solution to your problem, or the solution itself, before it fades from memory. Kekulé, for example, jumped up when he realized that he had solved his problem conceptually and spent the rest of the night working out the full solution based on the dream insight.

Dreaming, and even daydreaming, is an altered state of consciousness, and as you come back to your usual waking self, you are crossing the gap between the waking world and the dreaming world. It is very common, as anyone who has tried to remember dreams can attest, for a dream to be perfectly clear when you first wake up, but after a few minutes of having shaken off sleep, to be completely forgotten. This is why it's important to write down your dream or answer right away.

Applying the Clue Lifecycle

The final stage that Rheingold and Harman identify is *verification*. This is very similar to our concepts of "confirmation" and "validation" in the stages of the Clue Lifecycle. For scientific problems, verification can be a straightforward process: you have either solved the problem or not. But for social or business issues, you will have to use the Clue Lifecycle to take *action* and find *validation*.

As we said earlier, clues usually give you a direction, and clues that come from dreams are no different. Occasionally, you may get a solution through your dreams that doesn't seem to be the right answer, or that doesn't seem to solve the problem in the way that you thought it would, or that you aren't sure is really a solution. In these cases, you have to follow the direction that the clue is giving you in order to find the next clue. Use additional synchronicity to guide you in the days to come.

The best way to verify a solution to a non-scientific problem that you've received from the dream state, or from a daydream or vision, is to keep an open mind. Usually, the vision will *suggest a direction* that you should follow, rather than simply suggesting a practical solution. This is particularly true when you are trying to make an important life decision.

By keeping an open mind throughout the day, you're setting yourself up to recognize that "funny feeling" that comes when the "invisible hand" points something out to you. It is that "odd sensation" which occurs when there is some synchronistic match between something you see or hear in waking life and what was in your vision. That's usually a signal to dig deeper.

A great fictional example of this is given in the 2003 movie, *The Last Samurai*. At the beginning of the movie, Katsumoto, the leader of the Samurai, is sitting and meditating on a grassy hill. He receives a vision—of a white tiger that is roaring at him. Later in the movie, he arrives at a battlefield to see all of the enemy troops dead or fled, except one—the American solider played by Tom Cruise. He has that "odd sensation"—you can see it in his eyes—as he watches Tom Cruise's character fight off a whole group of attackers, much like a tiger. As if that weren't enough, Cruise's character grabs a pole and uses it to defend himself. The pole contains one of the flags of the samurai—in this case a *white tiger*.

This scene, though fictional, is a great illustration of how synchronicity can be used to back up a dream or vision. The samurai decides at this point that he will keep the white man alive, honoring his vision. Note that the vision didn't tell him exactly what to do—it was just enough to jog him into (1) noticing the synchronicity when it happens, and (2) using the synchronicity to lead in some direction.

That's a perfect example of how clues work. One clue leads you to the next, which leads you to the next. Follow the clues and you will find the treasure.

Bridging the Gap between the Worlds

In looking at each of the examples given at the beginning of this chapter, I can't emphasize enough the last item in the analysis: *the importance of acting on your dreams.*

It is not enough to have dreams that *allude* to some events in waking life. To become effective at using your dreams to solve problems in the real world, you have to learn to bring the energy of the dreaming state into the waking state and vice versa. This is done, as mentioned in other chapters, by *honoring* your dreams. This means to take some action that was precipitated by a dream.

The best way to do this is to do something physical with the memory of the dream. This could be simply sketching out a picture of some place or thing that you saw in a dream. If Salvador Dali hadn't attempted to draw the surreal pictures of clocks melting that he saw in his dream world, he might not have been as successful or as well known today. If Gandhi hadn't acted on his dream of *peaceful civil disobedience*, there might have been much more bloodshed during the Indian revolution.

Taking action is key to bringing the knowledge and

wisdom of the dream state into waking life. The more that you "honor your dreams," the shorter the gap will become between your dreaming state and your waking state. This means that you'll find it easier to use the power of your dreams to help you solve everyday problems and to help you in making major decisions in your life.

Of course, the key to problem solving using your dreams is to bring some aspect of the problem you're trying to solve into your unconscious when you fall asleep.

Watching the Pattern Unfold

Of course, you shouldn't limit yourself to the sleeping or reclining state when receiving answers to your problems. As you start to "settle into" a rhythm for asking for solutions, don't forget to pay attention to synchronicity during your waking life.

The "invisible hand" is always at work, and is often pointing out clues without us being aware of it. In fact, as we have seen, these "funny feelings" often come when we are scratching the surface of a pattern that is emerging in our lives just beneath the surface. This pattern often involves more than the task at hand; it usually involves the unfolding of various threads that are weaving themselves together into a long-term life and career path that we may only be dimly aware of at the time.

EXERCISE

Asking for Solutions to Your Problems

You can use these methods to solve problems in your life, career and work, through your dreams or signs. The key steps to remember are:

- **Asking for a solution.** This can be done consciously by writing a problem down, or unconsciously by simply concentrating on it throughout the day for several days. It is important that you do this enough times that a mental impression is made. Once that happens, your unconscious mind will get to work on the problem.

- **Incubating.** You need to move yourself into the correct state to receive an answer. This may be a dream, or it may be a vision you receive while in a relaxed state, or it may be from some set of clues or synchronicities in the waking world. Usually this means letting go of the problem once a mental impression is made. This is not so easy to do, but may be an important part of the process. If you have been thinking about the problem all day, write down your question and then forget about it for a bit. The idea is to get your conscious mind out of the equation to allow your "Eureka!" moment to come through.

- **Illumination.** If you have asked for a solution and "let go," you may end up with your "Eureka!" moment at an unexpected time. When you receive an insight, vision or dream that "feels" like it's relevant to your problems, write it down in your Book of Clues.

- **Verification or confirmation.** If the message is clear, you may be able to move quickly to an objective verification. If the message isn't so clear, you need to keep an open mind and use synchronicity to find a direction that you want to go in. Recognize that "funny feeling" which points out that something in your environment is relevant to your vision, and learn to follow that direction.

Although this is presented as a formal process, each person will run through these steps slightly differently. The key is to find your own rhythm, your own "rituals" for asking for solutions, and your own preferred way to get into a state of relaxation for answers to your life issues to come through.

Like many of the examples in this chapter, this may be through a dream while you are fully asleep and your conscious mind is more or less turned off. Or, like Archimedes, and even Leo Szilard, you might like to sit in your bathtub relaxed and let ideas and visions come to you.

Or you may find that the state between sleep and wakefulness—what I like to call the in-between state and what some refer to as the "Twilight Zone"—is the best way for you to be sufficiently relaxed for answers to come through without conscious interference. This "twilight zone" is particularly effective in my own life for solving problems. I often get the best ideas for writing and problem solving at work while I am waking up in the morning. The idea comes while I am only half-awake, and then I tend to rush out of bed, sit down at my computer and start writing.

Note that the conscious, logical mind is still needed, but more at the stage of "asking" and of "confirming" or "verifying" your answer. The actual illumination and incubation will happen in their own time. After a while you may even be able to learn your own preferred methods for incubation and illumination.

" It's a poor sort of memory, that only works backwards. "

–The White Queen
Alice in Wonderland, Lewis Carroll

PART IV

A STEP BACK

"Except ye see signs and wonders, ye will not believe."

–John 4:48

CHAPTER 10

Where Do Clues Come from? A Spiritual and Religious Perspective

While many traditions agree that clues (in the form of signs, synchronicity, coincidence, hunches, intuition and dreams) do exist, there are lots of different ideas about the origin and nature of these clues. Are they set up for us in advance, and if so, who sets them up? Or are they dynamically created, and if so, is there someone or some thing monitoring the clues? If there is a Treasure Map for our lives, where does it come from, and why can't we see it in its entirety?

In this chapter and the next, we will step back from the day-to-day part of the treasure hunt, and take a look at two very different viewpoints about the origin of clues and why they are important elements of our life on this planet.

In this chapter, we'll explore the *spiritual* perspective, which says that many of the major clues are set up for us in advance, and that they are there to remind us of the journey that we are *meant* to live in this life. In the next chapter, we'll explore a more *scientific* viewpoint, one that involves quantum physics.

Reincarnation, Past Lives and the In-between

Past lives, while still not accepted by the majority of Westerners, are a common model in the East for how we incarnate and reincarnate. In the West, this idea has become more popular over the last few decades, with the growth of interest in Eastern traditions including meditation and Yoga.

More recently, many psychologists and therapists who use hypnotic regression have found themselves inadvertently in the realm of past lives. When looking for the origin of a particular physical or emotional issue of a subject under hypnosis, they ask the subject to go back to the origin of the problem, and they unexpectedly find themselves in a subject's past life. Brain Weiss, MD, had such encounters and wrote his book, *Many Lives, Many Masters*, about numerous instances of this.

The thing is, you don't have to believe in past lives to acknowledge that somehow revisiting a trauma in hypnosis can clear up both physical and psychological ailments. Whether this past life actually existed or was some scenario that impressed itself in a patient's mind in relation to a specific ailment, the thousands of case studies of spontaneous healing occurring after revisiting a past-life trauma is undeniable, even to a skeptical engineer.

This book isn't about past lives per se, but one question about reincarnation that a small number of psychiatrists have stumbled upon in their regressions is that, if we incarnate multiple times, where do we go in between lives? While many regressions end up in past lives, only a few end up in the "in-between" place—where you end up after you die and where you stay until you are reborn. In his book, *Journey of Souls*, Dr. Michael Newton explores this "in-between" state in some detail, and there are similarities to descriptions given of the "after-life" by survivors of near-death experiences (NDEs).

Crossing the River of Forgetfulness

In this model, our *mission* or *purpose* in this life is usually given to us in that in-between place. Then we are sent off to incarnate as a baby, where we promptly forget what we are here to do as we struggle with more immediate concerns like walking, crying, eating, etc. By the time we are old enough to venture out on our own, many of us are just struggling to make a living, and if we are lucky, might remember only bits and pieces of our mission.

In some Buddhist traditions, the process of incarnating requires crossing the "River of Forgetfulness," where we forget all about our past lives and the intent, mission, and karma we are here to fulfill in this life.

Similarly, in Chinese mythology, the goddess Meng Po is the Lady of Forgetfulness, and she brews up a Tea of Forgetfulness for us, that we drink just before incarnating. This helps us forget our past lives so that we can have a "fresh start." Unfortunately, it also causes us to forget our memories of the "in-between" place as well, including our mission for this life.

Sometimes, every now and then, we are given a direct glimpse of what the mission in our lives, our life's work is. Winston Churchill was said to have told a friend when he was just a boy that one day he was going to be called on to save the British Empire.

For most of us, we don't get a direct vision or message of what we were meant to do in life. In fact, we might not be sure, but we usually have hunches and guesses. We get little glimpses of things that draw our attention: interests, activities and people that bring us joy. These are the little clues that are placed for us along the way, like breadcrumbs leading us on a cosmic treasure hunt, back to the place and person we were meant to be in this life.

CASE STUDY NO. 37:

Coming Back for a Purpose—the Curious Case of Dannion Brinkley

While most of us only get glimpses of what we are here to do, in some cases our lives are so off track that we must be given a serious wake-up call.

A great example of this is the experience of my friend, Dannion Brinkley, who was struck by lightning in 1976 and was declared clinically dead. He had a near-death experience (NDE) before the term was widely used. He wrote about it in his bestselling book, *Saved by the Light.*

After going through various stages of being on "the other side" (including a panoramic 360-degree life review, where he saw the results of his actions on every single person he'd ever dealt with), he was told by Beings of Light that he "had to go back."

In *Saved by the Light*, Dannion writes:

> Then the Being let me know what I was supposed
> to do back on earth. I was to create centers where
> people could come to reduce stress in their lives.
> Through this reduction of stress, said the Being,
> humans would come to realize "as we do," that
> they are higher spiritual beings. They would
> become less fearful and more loving of their
> fellow man.[1]

Then Dannion describes what they showed him: a vision of seven rooms, each with different steps and technologies (including biofeedback machines and what can be described as a space-age bed) to help people reduce stress and get to the other side. He wasn't shown exactly how to build each component, though, and this made him nervous.

When he saw the complexity of the centers and protested that he didn't know enough about all of the topics covered to build this kind of facility, he was told by the Being: "Don't worry. It will come to you."

I met Dannion almost 40 years after his near-death experience. Since he had come back, he had become a bestselling author and had started several organizations to help with end-of-life care and hospice work (where his experience was invaluable), and though he had seen the centers again in his second near-death experience (recounted in his second book, *At Peace in the Light*), he was *still* working on fulfilling that mission, tinkering with the space-age beds.

Setting Up Clues for Ourselves in Advance: Major Clues

Most of us aren't given a direct experience or message like Dannion was. If you don't know what your work is or what you are meant to do, my advice to you is: *Don't Panic!*

Remember what the Beings of Light told Dannion: "It will come to you."

Your job is to simply recognize the clues when they come to you, *even if you don't have any idea what the clues will be in advance.*

Like Dannion, there are many who believe that since we have to cross the River of Forgetfulness, the powers-that-be also give us clues to guide us toward that mission. Sometimes these clues are set up in advance—i.e. before we are born—and at other times they are course corrections along the way. I call the first set, *major clues*, and they include the people we are meant to be with in our lives, as well as the major decisions we are here to pursue.

Brian Weiss, MD, has used past-life regression techniques with thousands of patients, often finding that specific ailments disappear when light is shed on the origin of these conditions. Although a discussion of healing ailments via past-life regressions is beyond the scope of this book, Dr. Weiss also found, across his many regressions, that there was a pattern to our lives that gets set before we are born, and that "clues" are placed in our path to help us recognize these. In his book, *Messages from the Masters*, Dr. Weiss writes:

> There is considerable evidence that we actually see the major events in the life to come, the points of destiny, in the planning stage prior to our births. This is clinical evidence, gathered by myself and other therapists from our patients who have experienced pre-birth memories while under hypnosis, during meditation, or through spontaneous recall. Mapped out are the key people we will meet, our reunions with soul mates and soul companions, even the actual places where these events will eventually occur. Some cases of *déjà vu*, that feeling of familiarity, as if we have been in that moment or

that place before, can be explained as the dimly remembered life preview coming to its fruition in the actual physical lifetime.[2]

A Counseling Session before Embarking

After stumbling upon the "in-between state" numerous times, Dr. Michael Newton—who holds a doctorate in counseling and has done thousands of regressions—wrote in *Journey of Souls* about what he found. Dr. Newton has also come to believe that we have a life-planning session with the equivalent of a "spiritual counselor" before we choose a specific life.

He describes a planning room where we meet with our counselor, who might be an advanced Being of Light (or just someone more advanced than us), to choose the general outline of the life that we are planning to live, and then we see major events on a sort of projector.

This projector shows some of the general circumstances and major events of this life, and we can watch these as we would watch a recording, speeding up or slowing down the projector at specific instances. This projector is also capable of showing parallel lives or alternate lives, depending on some of the choices we make. In *Journey of Souls*, Dr. Newton presents transcripts of sessions where the hypnotized patient remarks that their life is presented on a master screen with colored lines of energy. The "dots" or connecting points of these lines are usually major life decisions and the soon-to-be-born soul (i.e. us) can move forward or backwards.

Using this "spiritual time-travel device," as I like to

think of it, the soul can also see past lives clearly, reflecting on the missions and the lessons learned from them before embarking on the new life. We'll talk more about "alternatives" in life in the next chapter as we discuss parallel worlds.

Our mission generally might involve helping people of a certain type or contributing to the world in our own unique way. There are always specific people, places and circumstances that we are meant to be with and to experience, and it's important that we do not ignore these people, places and circumstances as they appear in our lives.

How will we recognize these people, places, and circumstances if we cross the "River of Forgetfulness" when we are born?

In *Journey of Souls*, Dr. Newton goes into some detail about the "embarkation session" where our guide reminds us of the major clues that we are to look for in the following life, in case we forget. "Although amnesia does prevent having full conscious knowledge of this plan, the unconscious mind holds the key to spiritual memories of a general blueprint of each life."[3]

Since the unconscious holds this general blueprint, whenever a clue comes along that moves us toward or away from this blueprint, it notifies us. How? Through funny feelings, emotions, sensations, dreams and more! This is why clues are very subjective—the things that set off my unconscious about my general purpose in this life are very different than those which might set off yours.

Cramming before Incarnating

Dr. Newton goes further and says that we don't just select a life; we coordinate with other members of our group who are going to play significant roles in our life.

> Using the analogy of life as being one big stage play, we will have the lead role as an actor or actress. Everything we do in the play affects other minor characters (minor because they are not us) in the script. Their parts can be altered by us and ours by them because script changes (the result of free will) can be made while the play is in progress.[4]

In many of Dr. Newton's interviews, the subjects recall that the last step before coming back into this life ("incarnating") was a form of "recognition class." In this class, different souls that are going to have significant encounters with each other in the coming life are reminded of certain *triggers* that they can use to recognize each other. When incarnated, after we have gone through the River of Forgetfulness, it can be difficult.

What are these triggers? They are very similar to what we call *clues* in the ultimate treasure hunt. One subject, S, during hypnosis explained to Dr. Newton:

> S: The signs are placed in our mind now in order to jog our memories later as humans.
> **Dr. N:** What kind of signs?
> S: Flags—markers in the roads of life . . .

> The road signs kick us into a new direction in life
> at certain times when something important is
> supposed to happen ... and then we must know
> the signs to recognize one another, too.[5]

The subject is describing two types of major clues—those that tell us to go in a certain direction in life, and those that help us to recognize the other significant players.

These clues, explained the subject, are "small details"—not like the "major life preview" that occurred earlier with the "spiritual time-travel device." These small details will trigger certain feelings in the subject's mind, almost like a post-natal suggestion (i.e. something that the subject will remember after they are born when they see a certain trigger).

In the case of subject S, he was supposed to meet his soul mate, and the signs were that he would meet her on the "street on a bicycle ... she's wearing a silver pendant" and that he (S) must ask her about her silver pendant. Later, he reveals that his wife-to-be will be named Melinda and it's her laugh that he must recognize.

> S: When we meet, her laugh is going to ... sound
> like tiny bells ... chimes ... I really can't describe
> it to you ... Then the scent of her perfume when
> we first dance ... a familiar fragrance.[6]

The "recognition" is the internal feeling that comes with an "external cue." Many of us may be familiar with the ideas presented here for people who are soul mates, or meant to be our partners in this life. The same goes for good friends and buddies, though the recognition may not be as glaring.

OK, How about Western Religions?

OK, so we've looked at a model that's believed in by many spiritually oriented people and based on the Eastern religious idea of reincarnation.

I was surprised to discover, well after I was into the process of looking for and following my own clues, that many of the Western religions, including Islam and various sects of Christianity, have their own beliefs and model about clues and how they occur. These usually involve getting signs from God or from angels.

CASE STUDY NO. 38:

Asking for a Sign in the Islamic Tradition: *Istikhara*

A few years ago, my brother moved back to Pakistan and met a girl he wanted to marry. They asked her father for permission, but he was hesitant because it would mean that his oldest daughter would move to the United States, far from the rest of her family. Instead of answering right away, her father said that he wanted to do *"Ishtikhara."*

I had never heard of this term but when my brother described it, it sounded a lot like he wanted to wait for a "clue."

Basically, he would offer a prayer and ask God about a difficult decision he needed to make. In this case, it was letting his oldest daughter marry my brother. After asking God for the answer, he would wait over a three-day period for a sign as to what he should do. It sounded a lot like the concepts we are talking about here in *Treasure Hunt*, asking the universe to send you clues to where you should go next, but coming from a more traditional religious context.

As I looked into this more, I realized that *Ishtikhara* is a fairly well-known procedure in the Islamic world. In fact, traditionally you would ask God a question before you went to sleep, and then you would wait for an answer in your dreams over the next three nights. Over time, this tradition has expanded to include looking for signs and portents during your waking life. This tradition has a lot in common with "Incubating a Dream," an exercise that we explored in Chapter 9, "Problem Solving and Creativity from Dreams: Not Just for Old, Dead People."

Asking for a Sign in the Mormon Tradition

A few years ago, I gave to a Mormon friend a copy of my book, *Zen Entrepreneurship*, in which—drawing from my own story of starting and growing my first company—I talk a lot about clues as "messages from the hidden worlds."

I didn't know much about the Church of Latter-day Saints, and since the book was about my personal exploration of Eastern traditions, such as meditation, I fully expected that he might not resonate with the themes in the book which included my own story of looking for clues.

To my surprise, when I saw him a year or two later, he said that there were things in my book which were similar to some of their beliefs in the Church of Latter-day Saints (or LDS for short).

He gave examples of two terms in particular—*inspiration* and *revelation*—both of which tie very closely to our ideas of "Big" and "little" clues. An inspiration, he explained, was when you had a little impulse to go and talk to someone or call them. Usually, he said, members of the Latter-day Saints are encouraged to follow these "inspirations" because they could be a message from a higher power that you have something to do to help this person, or vice versa.

He gave the example of being at a friend's house when a female LDS member knocked, selling cupcakes door to door, which his friend didn't buy. As soon as the person left, he felt an inspiration to eat some cupcakes, a hankering that doesn't happen often. He went out after the woman selling the cupcakes and started talking to her. By following this clue, he found out that she was having trouble with her faith and life, and he was in a position to help. This was a perfect example of following a clue, a hunch, or as he refers to it, an inspiration.

Revelations, on the other hand, are big messages in the Mormon tradition, such as "I had a revelation that I should move to another city" or "another job." These are like our "Big Clues" that come to a person with a clear message. Like our "Big Clues" and "Big Dreams," revelations in the LDS tradition don't usually need to be interpreted. They demand to be followed.

Coincidence and Synchronicity in the Bible Belt: Messages from God or Guardian Angels?

I was on a radio show a few years ago hosted by a woman from the South, an area of the U.S. known informally as the Bible Belt. Again, I was a little nervous because the philosophy in my books tends to lean toward Eastern concepts. I was surprised when the host said that she often had to translate some of the terms into more traditional Christian language, but that when she did that people in the Bible Belt were essentially accepting of these concepts. In particular, she said, they were very open to the idea that we are guided by higher forces. As long as we referred to these higher forces as *angels* and/or God, and not as synchronicity or the universe, they were very consistent.

This was perhaps best expressed by SQuire Rushnell, a former television executive, in his bestselling book, *When God Winks at You*, in which he, like people in other spiritual traditions, expresses the belief that coincidence and synchronicity are really messages from God. Rushnell says, "Every time you receive what some call a coincidence or an answered prayer, it's a direct and personal message of reassurance from God to you—what I call a *godwink*."[7]

When I first heard about his book, I realized that what Rushnell calls godwinks are pretty similar to what we call *clues* in this book. Sometimes they are clues pointing you in a certain direction, and sometimes they are meant to be a confirmation or validation of a direction you're already on in your life.

In Christian (and many non-Christian) traditions, there is the concept of "guardian angels," who are assigned to us to watch and protect us. As in the famous movie, *It's a Wonderful Life* with Jimmy Stewart, these angels are trying to direct us when we get "off-course" in our lives. How do they do that? Since they don't normally appear to us in person, as in *It's a Wonderful Life*, they have to send us message in other ways—clues that catch our attention so that we might know what to do next!

Recognizing the Clues and Following the Map

One thing I learned at MIT was that most of what we call *science* is really a series of models about how the universe works. The underlying "True Nature of Reality" is far too complex to put into words or mathematical equations, but we can create models that approximate to the "True Nature of Reality." These models are to be held on to as long as they are useful.

Each of the traditions explored in this chapter presents models of reality—of how and/or why your personal Treasure Map exists and why you are attuned to clues related to your personal treasure hunt.

In one model, which we've explored in this chapter, they come not from the unconscious as much as from the pre-conscious, from the place before you were born, the place in-between life and death. We set ourselves up to meet certain people and make certain decisions, and to ensure that we don't forget, we set up these clues. This is a fascinating model of how clues work and what our Treasure Map is trying to guide us toward.

In another model, the more religious model, there are spiritual guides and guardian angels who exist in another dimension, and they are constantly watching us and sending us messages as we need them. In yet another model, clues are actually messages from God, who wants to support you. In the Islamic model, there is even a formal term, *Istikhara*, for asking for guidance from God.

I find that while all of these models have their pluses and minuses, they are also essentially saying the same thing. Whatever your beliefs, I encourage you not just to keep an open mind about where your personal clues may come from, but to go with whatever model seems best to you.

If you are someone who has no interest or belief in past lives or the in-between state, or even God or angels, you might want to look for a more scientific explanation of clues and where they come from. We'll explore this alternative "model" in the next chapter.

EXERCISE

Recognizing Pre-life Clues and Your Mission

This chapter put forward the idea that clues are *already set up for us, before we incarnate.* Although these clues are about "major" players in our lives (soul mates, business partners, best friends), the details are usually "small details" that stick in our minds and help us to recognize them.

Let's examine how this might have worked in the past and see if it can help us in the future. Take a deep breath, pull out your Book of Clues, and, when you have a few uninterrupted minutes, let's dig in:

1   Choose someone who has become important in your life. This could be a spouse or romantic partner that you've spent a long time with, or someone you knew only briefly but who made a big impact on your life.

   a. Think back to the time you first met them. What did you feel? Was there a sense of recognition? Did you feel comfortable with them right away?

   b. Was there any aspect of this person's appearance, manner or clothing that you felt drawn to? It could have been their laugh; the way they held themselves, blinked; their nail polish or perfume; or even something they said.

   c. Now ask yourself: could this have been a clue that you set up in advance? If so, did you recognize the clue or were you tempted to ignore it?

d.   Write down these clues as if they just happened to you today.

e.   Repeat this for someone who was important to your life in a different way (i.e. if the first person was a romantic interest, this one should be a non-romantic partner—it could be a best friend, mentor, enemy, etc.).

2   Now look at a major decision that you made about your life—it could be what city to live in, what career to choose, some sacrifice you made, a way of life you pursued, a life-changing trip you went on, where you went to college, etc.

a.   Think back to before you made the decision.

b.   Were there any clues that tipped you off about the decision? Maybe it was something you saw in a movie, or read in a book or saw in a dream.

c.   Write down these clues as if they had just happened.

d.   Could any of the clues have been set up for you in advance to make sure you went down one path as opposed to another?

"Our minds are time machines, able to sense the flow of possibility waves from both the past and the future."

—Fred Alan Wolf
in *Parallel Universes* [1]

CHAPTER 11

Where Do Clues Come from? A Scientific Perspective

Now that we've explored spiritual and religious models for clues and where they come from, let's take a look at a more scientific model: quantum physics. In this model, our conscious minds are picking up echoes of information not from past lives but from the future—to be more precise, from a probable future or parallel universe.

Let's Start with Science Fiction

Much of what eventually becomes science starts out as science fiction. Here are some examples of ideas that science didn't figure out until well after they'd appeared in science fiction: traveling to the moon, atomic bombs, video chat, even global communication via satellite.

One of my favorite scenarios related to communication with the future is from the sci-fi/horror director John Carpenter, in the film *Prince of Darkness*.

In the film, a team of physicists from Caltech is investigating a series of anomalies near a church for their professor. They have come to believe that the anomalous physical phenomena happening around the church are arising from something (or someone) buried in a unique relic in the basement of the church. The scientific team comes in to take measurements and form a theory about what this strange relic in the basement is.

Because it's a horror film, you know something bad is going to happen. It turns out that the relic in the basement is actually some kind of a prison, like an ancient phantom zone, and inside this prison is the *Prince of Darkness* himself. The team is in danger of setting him loose on the world . . . and if that occurs . . . well . . . you guessed it . . . something very bad will happen!

OK, that doesn't sound very scientific but this is where it gets interesting. One of the participants starts to have a repeating dream. Then, as the film progresses, we realize that other participants are also having the same dream. Eventually, the team realizes that the dream isn't just a dream, and what's important is not just the fact that they're all seeing the same thing. The communal dream is actually a message from the future, sent back to the team as a warning not to "unlock" the Prince of Darkness. They are seeing what would happen if the Prince of Darkness is released; their future selves are sending back this message to warn their past selves not to take a certain course of action!

The mechanism for sending the message is the often theorized but not yet found particle, the tachyon, which travels faster than the speed of light. The only catch is that the scientists in the present don't have a receiver for these messages.

Or do they? They don't have an artificial receiver; the only receiver they have that can get messages from the future is . . . their brain. And their brains interpret these incoming messages as dreams.

While this scenario is obviously science fiction, it brings up some very interesting concepts about the present, the future, and consciousness as the link between them. Could a scientific team send back messages to themselves to be received by the only instrument capable of interpreting these messages: their own brains?

The Flow of Time in Common Sense and Quantum Physics

Let's start with some common-sense problems with this scenario.

For one thing, if it was possible to send messages from the future to the past, then this would create the potential that the past can be changed. This creates a set of paradoxes that physicists hate, summed up by the *grandfather paradox*: if a person were to go back and kill their own grandfather, they would never be born. And if they are never born, how is it possible that they went back to kill their grandfather?

Even if you could send information from the *future* to the *past* rather than actually go back in time, you could essentially accomplish the same thing—change the past so that the future doesn't happen!

Most of us experience time in one way: flowing from the past to the present to the future. In this way, we often think of time as a river with a current that flows in only one direction. However, in quantum physics and in many mystical traditions, this view is seen as incomplete.

Time is one of the only *non-observables* in physics. Unlike position or length, which can be observed directly, the flow of time cannot be observed directly. Instead, we rely on external clocks and use them to measure time: the earth around the sun (years), the rotation of the earth (days), the cycle of the moon, the motion of a pendulum, the turning of gears, down to the atomic clocks that are used for very high precision.

If time only flowed one way, like the current of a river,

then the past would contain the causes of the present, and the past combined with choices made in the present would determine the future. This makes sense to us from the perspective of our everyday world. I made a choice to go to college at MIT in the past, which led to my eventual graduation and getting a degree from that university.

But in quantum physics, things are not so simple, particularly at the subatomic level. In quantum mechanics, the future is described not as a single point, but as a Quantum Probability Wave, which contains a set of probabilities of future outcomes. Which outcomes happen (and in fact, which steps are taken to get to those outcomes) is based on mental choices we make.

When a choice is made (for example to measure the location or speed of a particle), the most common description in quantum physics is that a probability wave is said to collapse and we get an actual event out of many *probable futures*.

How does this collapse occur? No one knows for sure, not even the quantum physicists.

However, physicist John Cramer postulated the transactional interpretation of quantum physics, in which all events that are possible are contained in an offer wave, a wave of probability based on the present moment. This offer wave travels forward in time from the present to the future.

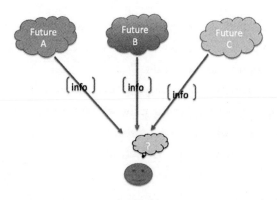

Figure 2: Information traveling from the future to the present before we make a choice.

In this model, there is then a corresponding echo wave coming from the future to the present, which is traveling backwards in time. When these waves meet, the points at which they "coincide" with high probabilities become points where the waves superpose with each other and a "real" event occurs rather than a "probable event."

This is a startling interpretation of quantum physics, where information is traveling not just from the past to the future, but raises the possibility of information coming from the future which can influence the present. In fact, it turns out there is nothing in the quantum equations which prohibits an event at time t2 from influencing an event at time t1 (which occurs before t2).

In his book, *Parallel Universes*, Fred Alan Wolf summarizes the flow of time: "The best picture, according to quantum physics, is that information flows in both directions simultaneously. The river of time has two counter-streaming currents. Information coming from the future as well as from the past influences the present."[2]

The Coincidence of Quantum Waves

As we mentioned earlier, in the strange world of quantum physics, it's difficult to know exactly where particles are at the subatomic level. That's why particles are described as having a probability of being in a certain location. It turns out it's impossible to know for sure multiple attributes of a particle—if we decide to measure its location, we can't know, for example, its exact velocity. On the other hand, if a scientist decides to measure the velocity, then it is impossible to measure the position exactly.

This is the essence of the *uncertainty principle*, first put forward by Werner Heisenberg. The particle is said to exist as a wave of probabilities of where it might be, until and unless someone decides to observe the particle. Then the probability wave collapses based on the *conscious* decision of the scientist concerning which aspect to measure.

In a well-known experiment, a photon is shot toward a screen with two slits in it. Using the normal definition of particle, a photon is a particle that should go through slit A or slit B. In this experiment, the photon displays properties of being a wave—meaning it goes through both slits at once—as well as being a particle—meaning it can only go through one of the two slits. This means that the photon is *both* a particle and a wave. Think of the wave as a set of probabilities of where the particle might be, and the particle as a concrete instance of a specific location the particle has been measured at!

What is the event that makes the probabilities collapse? It is the *conscious decision* of the scientist or observer. In fact, this is where the idea of an independent observer, so important in classical physics, completely breaks down in quantum physics. The observer cannot be separate from the experiment, because decisions made by the observer actually affect the experiment.

Therefore it is a series of *conscious mental events*, the choice and the observation itself, which determines how the probability wave collapses. This is a literal meeting of mind and matter—what conscious decisions we make actually changes the outcome in the physical world.

The real focus of these quantum waves propagating from the present to the future, as well as of probability waves migrating from the future to the present, is our mind. This was a startling conclusion for physicists, who were hitherto concerned *only* with external, observable phenomena.

The key to unlocking the information that travels back and forth in time from these quantum waves lies not in some technological device that physicists have yet to invent, but in our own minds and the way we think about things.

Again, Fred Alan Wolf in *Parallel Universes*:

> Every observation is both the start of a wave
> propagating outward toward the future in search
> of a receiver-event and is itself the receiver of

a wave which had propagated toward it from some past observation-event. In other words, every observation—every act of conscious awareness—sends out both a wave toward the future and a wave toward the past. Both the beginning of the wave and the end appear to begin in our mind—our mind in the future and our mind in the present.[3]

Essentially, the quantum waves traveling forward and backwards in time are messages from the future—from some mind in the future to our minds here in the present, as shown in Figure 2.

Parallel Worlds and Future Selves

Another way to think about "probable futures" is the *parallel worlds* hypothesis in quantum physics. It was put forward partly to explain away the paradoxes and issues that arise from the idea of information traveling from the future to the past (or with physical time travel to the past).

Let's return to the grandfather paradox. In the parallel worlds hypothesis, if you travel back in time and change the past you would then be on a different timeline from the one that you were on before. This new timeline is like a parallel world, where everything else is the same, except that your grandfather might never marry your grandmother, and your parents may never be born, which means you may never be born. The timeline is consistent with itself, but may not be consistent with other timelines (like the one that you started in).

The parallel worlds theory was put forward by Hugh Everett in 1957 at Princeton, under John Wheeler, one of the pioneers of quantum physics, and later championed by many others in the physics community, including Bryce DeWitt.

The theory was that every time a quantum decision has to be made—for example, if an electron has been shot toward a screen with two slits in it, A or B—we can't know for certain which slit it has gone through until we measure it. In the parallel worlds, or multiverse hypothesis, every time there is a quantum decision to be made in the subatomic world, the universes branch—and there is one universe where the electron passes through slit A, and one where the electron passes through slit B.

These universes exist independently of each other, but we don't know which of the two universes we are in until we make a conscious observation using our mind. If this happens with every major decision, we start to see different timelines involving the same particles but with different futures.

If we bring this up from the level of the subatomic particle to the world of everyday events, what does this mean? It means that every decision we make results in a branching off of two universes, as shown in Figure 3. This also resolves the grandfather paradox, because the killing of a person's grandfather results in a new branch, a new timeline. In this interpretation, some physicists believe that there are an infinite number of universes, each branch resulting from each quantum decision. Others believe that there are a fixed number, and physicists refer to this as the *multiverse.*

DeWitt says: "Every quantum transition taking place on every star, in every galaxy, in every remote corner of the universe, is splitting our local world into myriads of copies of itself."[4]

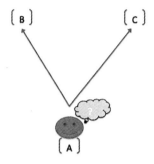

Figure 3: Branching occurs when you make a choice, creating parallel realities.

Timelines and the Multiverse

The multiverse theory brings us a resolution of the grandfather paradox, and a great many other paradoxes which might result from either receiving information from the future, or physically traveling back in time to change the past. Each branch creates a different timeline—in one timeline, the time traveler is born, and in another, he isn't.

For fans of science fiction, there are many dramatizations of the multiple timelines theory. In an episode of *Star Trek: The Next Generation,* the entire crew of the *Enterprise* is dressed differently than we are used to, and they are in a war of epic proportions against the Cardassians (not Kardashians!), which was not part of the "normal" timeline we followed in the series. As the episode progresses, we learn that the *Enterprise D* changed the past by helping a crew of an earlier *Enterprise (the Enterprise C)* to survive when they were supposed to sacrifice themselves as part of a battle. The outcome of that battle resulted in a ripple effect, and a new timeline was created.

How does the crew of the Enterprise know that they're in a different timeline? This is the same problem introduced in nearly every multiple timeline story and the multiverse in general.

In this *Star Trek* episode, there is an alien, Guinan (played by Whoopi Goldberg) whose mind conceives that something is wrong. She gets only hints, hunches and intuitions that things are not the way they were supposed to be. In other words, she gets clues.

If there were multiple universes happening all around us, how would we know? Like in the *Star Trek* episode, we might only know through some sort of hunch or intuition in our minds. Even though each universe might be physically separate, there is still something that links us together with other versions of ourselves, including our future selves and parallel selves.

Future Selves and Clues in the Ultimate Treasure Hunt

In our model of life as a treasure hunt, clues arise when we have a conscious mental reaction to observing some piece of information or some external event. It's very possible that the clues are coming to us from "probable futures" which are telling us to "pay attention" to one thing over another.

How do we make decisions that will affect the future? One explanation of the theories presented in this book is that there are future selves, perhaps multiple selves, who are sending us messages, as in Figure 2. Whether we tune into those messages or not depends on how we are using our minds and our intuition in the present.

This brings the explanation of synchronicity and clues out of the realm of religion (that signs come from God) or spirituality, and into the word of quantum physics (albeit with strong metaphysical overtones).

But if there are an infinite number of future selves, based on every decision we make, sending a probability wave back in time, then which ones are we tuning into? One answer is that it could be an arbitrary one. Another explanation is that it's one that is most *meaningful* to us at this point.

Meaningful is, of course, a subjective term, and it was used by Jung to define synchronicity as a meaningful coincidence, in order to bridge the gap between our subjective mind and some objective reality that we can't see. Quantum physics and the idea of future selves communicating with us seems to agree with Jung—that our minds are the transceivers of something that seems subjective but is actually part of a larger objective reality.

Clues in this context are messages from our future selves. More significant clues are messages that we should move in a particular direction when faced with a major decision. Just as clues are very subjective, so too are potential futures and the information that we get from them. According to this interpretation of quantum physics, we receive subjective information and the future that we travel to is the one we pay most attention to in our minds in the present!

Consciousness, then, is the critical factor in both recognizing clues and getting messages from the future in your treasure hunt as well as in the quantum model of waves of information traveling in both directions in time. Whichever choice we make causes a fracture in the universe. Are these fractures permanent? Not necessarily.

Branching and Merging

I would suggest that rather than having universes branch off at every single decision point, it's the major decisions that we make which determine alternate futures. For example, if John marries Lisa and lives in California, he might go down Path A in life. If John marries Sangita and moves to Bombay, he might go down a completely different path, Path B in life.

On the other hand, if John has eggs or oatmeal for breakfast today, this may not be such a consequential decision since he will go to work after breakfast and make other decisions which may not make any difference on his larger path through life—he may still be on Path A or Path B.

If we stick to the quantum mechanical explanation (only for the moment, though, since I believe it's incomplete without also tying into a more metaphysical or spiritual model of what we are here to do), this means that even though a decision was made (eggs vs. oatmeal) and universes may have branched, they come back together.

This is the fundamental branching structure of the matrix that is our life and which determines our future, shown in Figure 4. Not only do we branch, but it's possible that the branches merge back together.

Using a more metaphysical description, if John didn't talk to Sangita at the airport and didn't get to know her then, it's possible he might have run into her at a physics seminar at the university they were both studying at, so there's still a chance that they may get married.

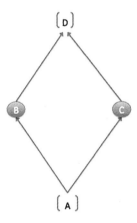

Figure 4: Fundamental branching and merging.

Figure 4 shows how this fundamental branching and merging happen. If you start at point A, you make a choice to go to either point B or point C. At either point B or C, it's possible to make a choice to get back to D, in which case the universes merge, and we are back at point D.

A slightly modified version of this image came to me in a deep meditation as I was exploring the concept of parallel lives and the minor and major choices we make in life.

It's also possible to take a broader view—where point A is our birth and point D is our death. Points B and C in Figure 4 represent different paths we might take in life, but we may end up at the same point, despite these choices. This now starts to look like our spiritual explanation in the previous chapter—where our life has some large plan or pattern—where we were meant to experience certain things, meet certain people, make certain contributions, but the ways in which we get there may vary.

If we take that fundamental branching diamond, and expand it out into a larger pattern (see Figure 5) and assume either that each branch point is a single, small decision, or that each fork is a major decision, you can see that the pattern becomes more complete, but it's also possible that we arrive at the same point even though we may make different decisions.

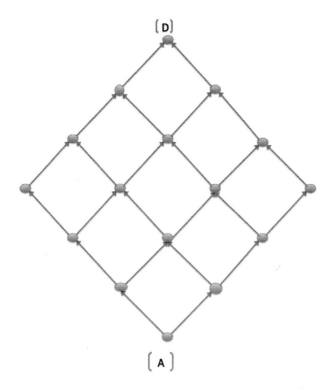

Figure 5: Branching and merging: traversing through life.

In this expanded picture, what we see is a network of possible presents and futures . . . if we consider Figure 5 to be a zoomed-out version of Figure 4, then points A and D can still be birth and death, with myriad choices in between.

The path that we traverse from point A to D can vary, based on our decisions in this life. But it's also possible to end up in the same spot, even though we follow two different paths. This is illustrated in Figure 6, where the dashed and solid paths represent different decisions made, different life lessons learned, but both start at point A and end up at point C. This is an example of where the worlds branched and then merged irregularly but you still get to the major life point at C, which then leads to point D, the point of death.

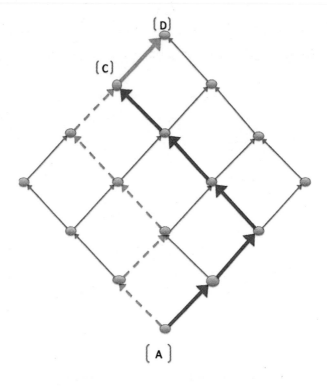

Figure 6: Two different paths lead to the same place.

The Path from the Past to the Future

In this chapter, we have explored a different way of thinking about clues. Using models that come to us from quantum physics, *clues* might literally be "messages from the future." To be more precise, messages from our "future selves."

If this is the underlying nature of reality, then science may have an explanation for where clues come from and why they leave such interesting conscious imprints on us. Our feelings are still the key, because they determine what our mind focuses on at the moment. Quantum physics tells us that of all possible futures, the one that we experience is the one that we pay attention to the most.

As we look into this further, the model of parallel lives becomes interesting because it tells us that all possible futures may exist, some with more probability than others. Each time we make a significant choice, we might be picking a path through all the possible branches of this life. Since most decisions won't alter our life path, these parallel universes merge back into one very quickly. However, major decisions may take us on different paths through the "matrix" of life.

This gives us an even more intriguing idea of where clues may come from. Not just from the future; we might also be glimpsing our parallel lives, and the choices our parallel selves are making. This model of clues being "glitches" in the quantum Matrix, where our mind catches a glimpse of our future and/or our parallel selves, is an intriguing one and could fill a whole book on its own.

For the purposes of our personal treasure hunt, it gives us even more reasons why we should pay attention to clues. Our personal Treasure Map may really be a map through all the possibilities of our lives!

EXERCISE

Communicating with Your Future Selves

This chapter put forward the idea that the past and the future are not as fixed as we might think. With multiple probably realities (some more likely than others) in our future, it's possible that these events (a future self) might be sending messages back to us. Clues as we use them in this book could be called "messages from the future."

1   Work with a clue as if it were from the future.

    a. As you write down clues in your book, find a clue that has repeated itself and that you find intriguing. This could be a simple hunch, an intuition, even a minor vision of something—like the kind of decoration you might put up at a certain place in your house.

    b. Now let's play a game of "what-if?" What if this clue were sent to you by one of your probable "future selves"? Suspend disbelief for a moment while you consider this "possibility." If a future self were to send you this message now, which was picked up by your unconscious, what would that future self be saying to you?

    c. What would be the circumstances in which this future version of you is sending you this message? Would it be a deliberate message they are sending you (i.e. "make this choice, not that one," or "don't give up on X yet")?

2   Connect with your future self.

   a. Let's do a visualization of your self. Start by lying back on a couch and getting comfortable.

   b. Set the intention in your mind that you are going to find a future self that is more successful than you are right now.

   c. Put your right hand on your solar plexus—and watch your breathing for a few minutes. This has the effect of calming the nerve center (which is there physically) and the chakra (which is there energetically). If your mind is still not calm, put your left hand on your heart chakra. This is called the "tiki" pose, because so many statues have been found in the Pacific with hands on the heart and solar plexus.

   d. Visualize yourself in the river of time . . . your boat slowly moving forward. On either side of the river are probable future selves. Now imagine you are able to find one of these probable futures that is calling to you.

   e. You jump off the boat and the river into the future and find your future self there. What does he or she say to you? What do they show you? Where do they take you?

   f. After a few minutes of this, bring yourself back and write down what you learned.

"You can't connect the dots looking forward; you can only connect them looking backwards. So you have to trust that the dots will somehow connect in your future. You have to trust in something—your gut, destiny, life, karma, whatever. This approach has never let me down, and it has made all the difference in my life."

–Steve Jobs
CEO of Apple Computer and Pixar

PART V

UNVEILING
THE MAP

"I want to know for what a man is preparing himself. That is what I read out of his dreams."

–Carl Jung

CHAPTER 12

The Tapestry Reveals Itself

Where the Clues Lead

In many of the examples thus far, it's been clear where the clues were leading: to taking action in a *particular direction*, or simply toward a *particular* way of thinking about some problem.

In reality, though, the course of action recommended by any given string of clues is highly subjective, and depends on how you *interpret* the clue. Just like the symbology of our dreams, the meaning of the symbols that emerge for a particular clue, whether it occurs in our waking life or in a dream, isn't always clear at the beginning, nor is the eventual direction that a clue will take us if we follow it.

This is why the Clue Lifecycle is presented not just as a single, linear set of stages, but as one or more circles. Sometimes you will interpret a clue, take some action, and then have another related clue, and you will need to go through the same cycle again with the new clue.

In Chapter 3, I told the story of thinking of an old friend, Mario, whom I hadn't heard from or thought about in many months. When he suddenly appeared at the beginning of a cold New England winter, it had a particular impact on our business; in fact, he convinced us to go to a conference in sunny Florida that proved to be critical to the launch and success of our business. It was also a path that I hadn't anticipated.

That's how *clues* often work. *You know that they're leading you somewhere, but it's not always immediately apparent where that somewhere is.* As in any good treasure hunt, one clue will lead you . . . to the next clue on your path.

Jung believed that synchronicities reveal an underlying pattern to the events that occur in our lives that we aren't consciously aware of. Sometimes, that pattern leads in a different direction than we would choose, logically, and the reasons for going in this different direction only reveal themselves over time. The reason we refer to the path of our lives as a Treasure Map is because we need to let the whole pattern emerge over time.

A *Star Trek* Tapestry

When I was growing up, one of my favorite shows was *Star Trek: The Next Generation*. This wasn't just because it was one of the first TV shows to have its own special effects budget, nor was it only because I was a fan of science fiction. I liked how the episodes often raised psycho-spiritual issues by disguising them in an easily understandable and socially acceptable format— science fiction!

One of my favorite episodes is called "Tapestry," and it's an appropriate metaphor for the underlying Treasure Map that may exist in our lives without us being fully aware of how the threads weave together.

In this episode, Jean-Luc Picard, captain of the *Enterprise*, has what can best be called a near-death experience. During this experience, he's given a chance (by our favorite omnipotent alien, Q) to go back and change anything in his life that he regrets. Well, given the chance, who wouldn't go back and change some of the things from our earlier life?

In his case, his brush with death is actually caused by a failure of his artificial heart, which was put in after a nasty episode when Picard was a young man. This artificial heart was installed when he, as a brash young officer, got into a bar-fight with a rather unpleasant alien who was several feet taller than him (a Nausicaan). During the fight, the alien stabbed the young Picard in the heart. The older, wiser part of Picard had always regretted getting into that fight, and now he is given a chance to go back and change his impulsive, youthful ways.

In the episode he jumps at the opportunity, goes back in time, and changes his brash, youthful behavior, avoiding the fight with the alien that resulted in his getting stabbed. But almost as soon as it happens, we get the sense that something has gone wrong. He immediately alienates his two best friends by his "reasoned, adult" behavior, which is rather uncharacteristic of the impulsive young Picard at that age.

Once the deed is done, Q brings him back to the present, and Picard thinks that he has taken care of a terrible mistake from his past.

But in the present, something is definitely awry. In this new version of the present, he is no longer the captain of the *Enterprise*. In fact, he is a mid-level career officer in astro-mechanics. Not that there's anything wrong with being in astro-mechanics, but it becomes clear that he has gone from being the person in charge, a respected captain of the ship, to becoming a *non-essential, not very respected* member of the crew.

He learns that his career has taken a very different

direction from the career of Picard as we know him. Because this new Picard had always "played it safe" in his youth, he never took the risks in this new timeline that he had done in the old. As a result, he never really stood out, and never gained the respect of his peers or lived up to his destiny or potential! One of his most famous career moves, taking command of the Stargazer when its captain was killed, never happened, and he never got promoted.

Understandably, Picard is devastated by this revelation that his career has taken a very different route from the life that he knew and was proud of.

At this point, the reason the episode is called "Tapestry" becomes obvious—Picard didn't realize how intricately the threads in his own life had woven themselves together into his current career and life position.

The point here is not that we shouldn't regret or try to change things we aren't proud of, but rather that our lives are like a tapestry, the result of multiple interweaving threads that are the result of choices we've made in our lifetime. It's not always possible to know, consciously, how these threads fit together. In this example, Picard pulled what he considered a "loose thread," but it unwove a number of other threads that were essential to his life's work.

Going back to our example of the quantum possibilities in Figure 5, we see that Picard thought he was ending up at one point in the matrix, but ended up at a different point in the grid based on the major life choices he made.

At the end of the episode, he is given a chance to go back to the original timeline, complete with the fight with the alien which ends in Picard getting stabbed and receiving an artificial heart. *Again. Ouch.* But this time, Picard gladly accepts his irresponsible behavior, since it had been part of his personality and youth, and things go back to normal, artificial heart and all, and we see the Picard that we know and love, in command of the *Enterprise* and living his destiny.

The Pattern Emerges over Time

We don't all have to do something as crazy as getting stabbed by an alien twice our size to experience this phenomenon. The threads of our life are weaving themselves together into our own tapestry, our own personal Treasure Map.

It's not always possible to know exactly where a particular experience will lead, nor is it always possible to see the underlying order of the tapestry of our lives at the time. But if you follow the clues through multiple Clue Lifecycles—*intuition, confirmation, interpretation* and *action*—over a longer period of time, then you are on the right path to seeing this underlying order as it emerges . . . and it almost always does.

In Chapter 5, I told of my dream about starting a company in a new technology area, XML. Along with other clues related to this new technology area, this experience led my new company in a particular direction, and sometimes that's all that's important in a clue: that you start going in a particular direction, and see where it takes you.

While it held a specific clue about my company, this

dream also contained confirmation of and continued another thread in my life, which was about having my dreams and my spiritual experiences intertwined with my business experiences.

As with most Big Dreams, there were multiple levels of symbolism at play. First of all, one of my past mentors who appeared in the dream (which was clearly about the software industry)—a fellow named James—was actually one of my first meditation teachers.

Big Clues, including Big Dreams, and long strings of synchronicities that come with confirmation from the outside world, almost always deal with more than one thread in our lives.

In this case, the threads in my own life were entrepreneurship, writing, dreaming and spiritual growth, all of which were to interweave into a pattern that was unique to me, over a much larger period of time. Let's look at this another way.

Red Light, Green Light: When Obstacles Appear and Melt Away

Important clues always repeat themselves, often over a course of months or even years. This is why it's important to *write down the clues* as they happen. By writing them down, in addition to having a permanent record, the clue will make a stronger impression in our memories so that months or years later, when related clues appear (and they almost always do), you can recognize the new clue, not as an isolated event, but as part of a larger pattern in your own life.

Moreover, sometimes a door seems to open, with obstacles melting away (the Green Light); at other times, you take some action and it seems like the right action, but then things come to a halt (Red Light). This "Stop and Go" method of travel is very common for those who are following their own treasure hunt, and it usually means that the clues are showing you the right direction to go in your life, but the timing may or may not be right for you to pursue it. As a great metaphor, remember Sean Connery's character's "Grail Diary" in Chapter 2, which had clues collected over his entire lifetime, but it was only when his son, Indiana Jones, as played by Harrison Ford, was older that they were able to find the hidden location of the Grail.

Let's take another example.

CASE STUDY NO. 39:
Red Light, Green Light with My Writing

When I left my first company, Brainstorm Technologies, in 1997, I experienced a series of events that involved paying attention to internal and external clues. It began with a waking "intuition" that I should think about taking a trip to California. I was considering writing a book about some of the lessons I had learned in business.

Green Light

I had heard that finding an agent for a book was almost as difficult as finding a publisher; nevertheless, I decided to go ahead and look for one. I did a search on the internet and one of the first that caught my attention was in California—in Los Angeles. The "invisible hand" seemed to be pointing me to this one, for reasons that I couldn't guess at that time. I sent her an email, and within a couple of email conversations, in what seemed like an effortless process, she agreed to be an agent for the book.

I didn't realize that this was an example of obstacles melting away until friends in the publishing industry told me how difficult it usually is for new authors to get an agent.

When a clue or series of clues is leading you in a direction, and obstacles seem to melt away quickly, there's a pretty good chance that you're catching wind of an underlying pattern emerging in your life. The pattern may be a much larger one than you realize at the time— in fact the timing may take years for the full pattern to be revealed.

Within a rather short period of time, I found myself taking a trip to California for business reasons. The timing worked out well in that I could actually visit this agent in Los Angeles during the trip, which was originally to San Francisco.

During the meeting, we had a conversation about the book I had started writing, which was a practical business book with little or no spiritual dimension. When she asked me what other ideas I had, I told her that the book I really wanted to write someday would be about "synchronicity and business." She thought this was a great idea and wanted to know more about it. I hadn't particularly formulated the ideas consciously at that point, so only gave a brief overview.

"Why not write it now?" she asked. I told her that I

didn't quite feel qualified enough to write a book about the spiritual dimensions of business, even though I felt very qualified to write a book simply about start-ups since I had just spent the past few years running one

Secretly, I also wasn't sure what people in the "respectable" business world would think of me if I wrote about such topics. She found this amusing, and so we left the discussion at that point and went back to the "book at hand"—the practical book about start-ups that I had approached her about. She quickly agreed to become my agent for the book.

Red Light

Now, in an ideal world, this initial melting of obstacles ("Green Light") would continue to happen, and I would have written that book and had it published with no further ado. But we don't live in an ideal world—we live in a complicated world where threads are interwoven and the larger patterns don't reveal themselves right away but emerge over many years.

The interesting thing is that my heart wasn't really in the writing of that first book at the time, and within months it became clear that, for a variety of reasons, publishers weren't interested in another practical book about start-ups from a relatively unknown entrepreneur.

At first, I thought that my relationship with the agent in California had become a waste of time and was angry with her for not "selling my book." It wasn't until much later that I saw that this was part of a larger pattern that I needed to respect the timing of.

It was my own pattern related to pursuing interests in the business world. I was happiest, most fulfilled and successful when I was following my intuition, my dreams, and engaging in what I call "soulful" businesses, rather than simply "working to make money."

Green Light, Again

This pattern, which would unfold over many *years*, eventually evolved into the writing of the book on synchronicity and business that I first spoke about with my old agent in Los Angeles years ago—the book you are reading right now: *Treasure Hunt*.

More than 15 years later, I was in Los Angeles for a spiritual expo that I felt compelled to go to. As I was wandering around the expo floor, a booth with a lot of books in it caught my eye. This wasn't unusual, but I saw a book on synchronicity that jumped out at me, and as a result I struck up a conversation with the gentleman manning the booth. I asked him about the book and he casually mentioned that he'd like to have another book on synchronicity. I told him that I had already written a draft of a book on synchronicity, and he said that he was in charge of U.S. marketing and could get the book in front of his editorial group in London.

I had that kind of funny feeling that lets me know it's a clue. In this case, the clue was not just a synchronicity, but was literally about *synchronicity* (since the thing that began our conversation was an existing book about synchronicity, and where it led to was my book about synchronicity). To make a long story short, this clue led to the publication of the book you are holding in your hand right now, many years after I'd first come up with the idea of writing a book about synchronicity in business.

As I've mentioned numerous times, clues indicate direction, but they don't always indicate timing.

When Obstacles Appear and Melt Away

This brings us to the first of our next two Rules of Treasure Hunting:

TREASURE HUNTING RULE NO. 19:

When obstacles melt away, follow the "invisible hand"

To see this rule in action, let's look at another dramatic example of obstacles "melting away" for me, which occurred around the same time that I was visiting the agent in California.

Around the same time, I left my job as CEO of my first start-up, Brainstorm, and I had the intuition that I should move to California. This wasn't as easy as it sounded. This was at the height of the dot com boom, in early 1998, and housing was very difficult to find and extremely expensive in Silicon Valley. In fact, I was hearing horror stories of having to give your résumé before a landlord would consider you—and if you didn't currently have a job, which I didn't, it was unlikely you'd find a very good place.

During the same trip to California, I visited a friend from college who I hadn't seen in a while and told her I was thinking of moving out there, but I wasn't sure exactly how much I could afford to pay, or how long a lease commitment I was willing to make, or when I might actually make the move! Given the crazy environment there, these factors would *normally* have been disadvantages to my finding a smooth transition to California, either temporarily or permanently.

Coincidentally, my friend introduced me to one of her college friends whose roommate had *just* moved out, and so he was stuck with an extra, empty room. He was more than willing to rent it out on a month-to-month basis, and was very flexible on when I could move in. The apartment was in Mountain View, CA, the heart of Silicon Valley. The room was completely furnished already, so there was no need to buy any furniture, and most importantly, it was within an affordable price range!

At the same time, I learned that I was eligible for a severance agreement with my company, so I found myself with financial support for a number of months, the ability to move to California without selling my place in Boston, and the time I needed to think about what I really wanted to write and how.

Once again, my friends remarked how "surprised" they were that the "stars had aligned," and I was "led" to go to California for a six-month period without disrupting my life at all financially.

During the next few months, I was able to have the time to unwind, and to think seriously about writing about *business* and *spirituality*. I started very simply, writing down my own experiences about these topics in almost a story form, which later turned into my book *Zen Entrepreneurship*.

While there were many other coincidences that happened during this time, the point here is that the threads of *start-ups*, *writing*, *California* and *spirituality* were being interwoven into my own unique pattern that continues to unfold to this day.

When obstacles melt away, in a seemingly coincidental and synchronistic fashion, this is a *clue* in itself that the "invisible hand" is leading you in a particular direction for now.

At this time, there are several examples of "obstacles melting away" that occurred—one in finding an agent, which started me down the writing/publishing path, another in being led to a place to live, and the sudden income to support me while I was there—to help the pattern emerge.

Of course, the picture isn't always so rosy. Often, after a series of obstacles melting away (Green Light), you are likely to notice a series of new obstacles appearing in your way (Red Light). There is a corresponding Rule of Treasure Hunting to deal with that as well:

TREASURE HUNTING RULE NO. 20:

When obstacles appear, it is usually a matter of timing

Continuing my own example, in both cases, while obstacles initially melted away, they inevitably reappeared.

In the case of the agent, it was the difficulty I had selling the proposal for the original business book. In the case of my writing in California, after making significant headway on the book, I ended up moving back to Boston to start another company, and the book was sidelined for a few years.

In the unfolding of the threads that weave the tapestry of *your* personal and professional life, you will undoubtedly find yourself playing the Green Light–Red Light game as obstacles first melt away, and then a new set of them appear in your path.

Usually, when obstacles appear out of nowhere on a path that you were sure the clues were leading you on, it's usually time to slow down a bit. It's as if the "invisible hand" is saying, "Stop! This isn't the right timing for you yet."

These are both *essential* phases of a complicated pattern emerging over time—your personal Treasure Map. A pattern evolves from more than one single coincidence or synchronicity; it is rather the complex intertwining of multiple threads of your life that make the larger pattern.

In the "go" modes, it is clear what to do—follow through with the action pointed to by the clues. In the "stop" mode, you should do whatever you can, making perhaps smaller, more guarded progress, and go on with your life, waiting for the right timing to emerge.

In life, as in Hollywood, there really are no such things as "overnight sensations"—the most famous examples of these are usually individuals who have been working, bit by bit, on their careers for many, many years before they are finally "discovered." Many of us in the movie-going audience thought that Jim Carrey emerged out of nowhere as a major star after his movie *Ace Venture: Pet Detective*. But people in Hollywood had known Jim for years as a comic; no one, though, had found the right project to put him in.

The same will be true of the patterns emerging in your life … sometimes you have to keep making small progress, backing off and biding your time until the timing is right for the larger pattern to emerge.

CASE STUDY NO. 40:
A College Drop-out and Calligraphy

You don't always know when something that looks like a detour is actually a thread that will re-weave itself into the tapestry of your work and life in your Treasure Map. Let's take an example.

Steve, a California native attending college in Oregon, wasn't sure he wanted to continue his college studies, so one semester he dropped all of his college classes.

When he was walking along the road at the edge of campus, he noticed a flyer for a class on calligraphy. Something about this flyer intrigued the artist inside him, and he took the class, as a result falling in love with fonts and typefaces and all the variations of them.

Years later, when this young man, Steve Jobs, had become the co-founder of Apple Computer, and he was building the Macintosh computer, he remembered his passion for typefaces and insisted that fonts and typefaces were a key part of the new computer. Until then, most computers were green text on black background with only one font. The Macintosh opened up a whole new world of WYSIWYG (What You See Is What You Get) desktop publishing.

As far as he could tell at the time, there was no practical reason to take a class on calligraphy, except that it was "calling out" to him in some way. If it wasn't for the unexpected class on calligraphy, it's possible I might still be typing this manuscript on my computer in a basic green courier font on a black screen!

This is a great example of how our Treasure Map is revealed one step at a time; a clue from years ago might be the missing piece that you need in your life and work in the present.

Good Luck? Bad Luck? Who Knows?

The best advice I have concerning those times when it looks like obstacles are appearing on the path you thought you should be on is to remember the story of the old Chinese farmer, which I like to call "Good Luck, Bad Luck." I first read this classic story in an excellent book on synchronicity called the *Power of Flow*, by Meg Lundstrom and Charlene Belitz, and I paraphrase the story below.

An old Chinese farmer had a horse that one day ran away. His friends and neighbors came to him and said, "What bad luck you've had!" He smiled and responded simply: "Good luck? Bad luck? Who knows?"

Several days later, the horse returned, this time with a whole troop of wild horses, which the farmer took in. Now his friends said, "What good luck you've had to acquire so many horses!" His reply was once again, very simply: "Good luck? Bad luck? Who knows?"

While breaking in one of the wild horses, the farmer's son fell and broke his leg. Of course, the farmer's neighbors said something to the effect of, "What bad luck you've had that your son has broken his leg!" Once again, the farmer replied: "Good luck? Bad luck? Who knows?"

Soon thereafter, there was a war, and the soldiers came by and drafted every able-bodied young man in the village. Because the farmer's son had broken his leg, they passed him by and did not require him to join the army. Once again, the farmer's friends said something like, "What good luck you've had! Your son didn't have to go into the army!" Of course, once again, the farmer replied, "Good luck? Bad luck? Who knows?"

You can see where this is leading, and it is no different in our own lives.

One of the main points of the story is that during the emergence of a pattern in your life via a series of meaningful coincidences, you really can only see one part of the pattern at a time. What appears like an obstacle or a roadblock may in fact turn out to be something quite different when you look back upon it many months or even years later. In fact, many obstacles operate on *multiple threads* in our lives, and so can continue to unfold even after you think you have completed some phase of your life.

Where an Unhappy Accident Can Lead

This theme was reinforced in my own mind, and not altogether unrelated to one part of the story of the Chinese farmer, when I had a motorcycle accident in Bermuda in the summer of 2001. At first glance, this might seem like a stroke of "bad luck," especially since I was limping around for the rest of the summer.

But the law of unintended consequences was at work, and rather than sulking about the injury, I found that a pattern was emerging (or as the case may be, was *re-emerging*). The accident caused me to do two things.

First, I had to cancel my travel plans to go on an international trip for the second week of September that year. I just didn't feel like traveling internationally so soon after the accident—I needed time to recuperate. Given the mayhem caused by the 9/11 attacks on New York and Washington (including two hijacked planes that departed Boston, where I was living) that week, it turned out to be "lucky" that I wasn't traveling at the time.

Second, and most importantly, I found myself, as I stared at the pavement after the accident, contemplating how unhappy I was with my current position, so I started to think about what was really important to me in this life. I was left with the clear direction that I should go ahead with leaving the job I was in at the time—it wasn't fulfilling me either professionally or spiritually.

The impression was even more specific than that: I got a clear message that I should give myself some time and space for what was really important to me in life—not just keeping my current job or staying in my current business for the sake of making money. An "accident" tends to do that in your life—to cause you to re-examine your priorities about what is really important.

I acted on it within weeks. I enrolled in a series of classes on spirituality that I wanted to take in Miami later that winter, which I could not have made time for if I had stayed at that job. The "invisible hand" was already hard at work, and I didn't even know it. To this day, when my knee starts acting up, it's inevitably a clue to me that I'm probably unhappy with the direction/start-up/job that I'm doing and that I need to make more time for my spiritual pursuits.

Know When the "Invisible Hand" is at Work

The key to this process is to keep an open mind and learn to work with the circumstances as they evolve. At each step of the way in the unfolding of the path, noticing and following the clues that you write in your Book of Clues (which may come in the form of dreams, synchronicities, internal or external feelings) is the most important thing you can do.

When the "invisible hand" is at work, notice the clues that are appearing all around you and follow through with the process of the Clue Lifecycle. Only by following the clues will you be able to find your own "emerging pattern" that will tie together the life threads in your own personal tapestry: career, business and spiritual.

"'Your arrows do not carry,' observed the master, 'because they do not reach far enough spiritually.'"

–Eugene Herrigel
Zen and the Art of Archery

CHAPTER 13

Injecting Soul into the Soul-less Machine

Business as a Path of Personal Growth?

When I first tell people that I believe that business can be a path for self-expression and even spiritual growth, I often get funny looks. When I go on to explain why I think this is so, the funny looks often turn to looks of recognition as they recognize incidents from their own careers that reveal the "soul-less" nature of many corporations and the people that inhabit them today.

If you learn to pay attention to clues—signs, signals and messages—then the world of business can become more than a giant soul-less machine in which you are only a cog. If you learn to recognize when some aspect of your work, career or life path is truly "calling" you, then you too can recognize how the business world is an arena that can be used for personal expression and spiritual growth.

If you use your personalized Book of Clues to help you to navigate, your career path can unfold in a way that takes into account your strengths and weaknesses, and you can end up in the "right place" at the "right time." You will be on the way to finding your own personal definition of *true success*.

By doing these things as an individual, you can have a more fulfilling and successful career, can also impact on the corporate world as a whole, helping it to become more "soul-ful," to have more "integrity," and even contributing to healing some of the major issues that have been dogging our capitalist society recently.

Like the Native American cultures I spoke of earlier, you can see that dreams and waking synchronicities on each person's own treasure hunt can be used as the threads that connect the societal order to an individual's own gifts and ability to contribute.

As I mentioned in Chapter 1, when Dannion Brinkley "came back from the dead", he came to the conclusion that the world needed *Spiritual Capitalism,* as a situation where everyone is able to use their unique gifts to make a living. Utilizing your own gifts and making a contribution to the world is the real treasure in your own personal treasure hunt.

It is partly the absence of this view—that each person's path is unique and each has a unique gift to contribute—that has led to our current crisis of capitalism.

By crisis of capitalism, I don't just mean the turning of the business cycles or even the recent accounting scandals and the collapse of many Fortune 500 companies—though these are very important indications that something is wrong. I mean the lack of *soul, integrity* and *purpose* that many of us feel in our jobs and workplaces that lead to these kinds of symptoms. If we were all to follow our own personal Treasure Map to the real treasure, finding meaningful and fulfilling work, this crisis would start to abate.

Silicon Valley and Wall Street

During the dot com boom, I was often presented with business plans and asked to advise or invest in them because they were "guaranteed" to make money.

During those heady days, business plans were receiving millions of dollars of funding to exploit almost any emerging market opportunities. Even though I was right in the middle of it in many ways, I felt a discomfort at what was happening. This wasn't just because of the way in which money was being thrown around or made, or even because of the incomplete business plans that were being funded, but because of the significant number of new businesses, often with millions and millions in funding, that lacked "soul."

This funding, which was based solely on lofty "analyst projections" of growing markets, started with the growth of the internet, which fed the telecommunications industry and the "new economy," spurring the growth of the stock market in every sector. This huge wave of inflated wealth in turn led to the kind of behavior that initially brought down dot coms, then giants like Enron, WorldCom, and many others, later. It repeated itself to an extent in the Web 2.0 and real estate boom before the market crash in 2008. And as I write this, there is another cycle of millions being invested in soul-less companies pursuing the "next big thing."

During this time, too often, venture capitalists and market analysts would collude in deciding what the "next big" thing was and work with a group of "hired gun" entrepreneurs to "exploit" this market opportunity while the "window" lasted.

They would "analyze the market" and conclude that the next big opportunity was at the intersection of "X" and "Y." The analysts would then estimate that these markets would grow to $X billion in the next few years, and venture capitalists would put in tens of millions of dollars of funding to exploit this market opportunity.

I like to call this the "top down" approach to funding a new business—usually driven by individuals (analysts and venture capital firms) who speak the same language, often attended the same business schools, but very often had precious little actual business operating experience.

CASE STUDY NO. 41:
A Top down Approach to Starting a Company

This "top down" approach resulted in many, many "soul-less" businesses that were conceived from market charts and not from entrepreneurs who were trying to express some creative urge they had while making progress on their unique life paths—what I call a "bottom up" approach. We'll look at examples of that in a moment.

I remember a very well-known venture capitalist in Boston who decided to start up a company in the "MP3" space, because MP3 was the "next sure thing." The company looked around and brought together several individuals: a business guy, a technology guy, and a marketing gal (who was a friend of mine) who had some relevant experience with multimedia.

On the face of things, this might have seemed like a reasonable way to go. The VC firm gave them some money, put them into a room and told them to write a business plan, which they did, and which the venture capitalist subsequently funded.

The plan was put together in time *specifically* to get funding. Needless to say, the business had many issues. The founders didn't all get along, they couldn't agree on a particular vision for the business, and eventually my friend, the one who had the most experience with marketing multimedia products, left the company because of political disputes. The company, launched with a great fanfare, floundered quickly, even though it survived for quite some time because of the vast amounts of money the venture capitalist had put into it.

This was typical of the kind of "top down" business plans that were put together. It's not that these businesses can't be successful—some make quite a bit of money—but many, as in this example, flounder after an initial "bump." The problem with such businesses is not a "lack of money"—it's a lack of "soul."

Telling a Story—Top down or Bottom up?

I often like to use the analogy of what's happened in Hollywood over the past few decades to illustrate my point about the "top down" vs. "bottom up" approaches to business. Film studios, which have a certain amount of money to invest, want to put it into the next "sure thing." So, rather than taking a risk on a new or untried story, director or author, they simply regurgitate the formulas that have worked before.

As a result, moviegoers have been subjected to a flurry of drab sequels and "formulaic" movies that definitely qualify as "soul-less." Their sole purpose for being made was to *exploit* a market opportunity while it lasted—e.g. Fast and Furious No. 15, Super Hero Movie No. 10, etc. This has led to a growing recognition by many people that numerous "studio" movies aren't worth watching and that the "independent" movies are where the new, innovative stuff is really happening.

Contrast the way these "soul-less" movies are put together with the sometimes long and difficult process that more original stories go through to become feature films. Usually, there was a creator who wants to tell a story and so wrote a screenplay. Often, the experts didn't like the idea and rejected it because it didn't follow a well-known formula. The creator, however, believed in their stories so much that they stuck with them when times were tough, and eventually convinced enough people (within the studio or outside of it) to put up a small amount of cash (relatively speaking) to make the movies.

Oftentimes, these "innovative movies," like the original *Rocky*, the original *Terminator*, the original *Blair Witch Project*, and even the original *Star Wars*, went on to become some of the most innovative and successful movies of our time. However, as the sequels piled up, you could see the magic fading.

Each of these films were parroted numerous times by using a top down approach—"movies like X are successful, let's make another movie like X"—even to the point of creating terrible sequels made for multiple times the original budget.

The bottom up approach, where an author/creator/director is dying to tell a story, is not just a myth. It happens quite often in the world of movies and in the world of publishing. In many Native American cultures, the best stories were considered to have a life of their own, and would stalk a storyteller, crying out to be heard.

In this bottom up approach, the story becomes an

important reflection of the life and mind of a writer/ creator. The creative juices are called upon because the story is somehow tied to the individual life path, the emerging tapestry of that person, taking into account his or her strengths and weaknesses.

Successful books and movies are inevitably followed by sequels, which are usually made for ten times as much money as the original but are rarely as good except in the instances where they are an essential part of the original story. In fact, you might say that many of these sequels suffer from losing their sense of purpose, integrity and soul.

CASE STUDY NO. 42:

The Majesty of the Canyons of the Southwest

Let's take a look at a different way of doing business, a bottom-up approach that is more about the entrepreneur finding their way and wanting to make a contribution.

Let's look at another software company called Bryce, which developed software for producing 3D images and animations of realistic computer-generated landscapes, terrain, and even animation and fly-throughs. One of the original creators of this software, Eric Wenger, was the son of a geologist; while growing up he learned a lot about and became fascinated by *terrains* and *landscapes*. He later became an artist, doing graphical and 3D artwork, creating computer programs to help him along the way.

At a visit to a computer conference (called SIGGRAPH), he was drawn to a mathematician who was giving talks on algorithms for creating realistic landscapes, which he had been developing and publishing for a period of many years. The presenter was initially interested only in tools to help him produce the kind of art that he personally enjoyed.

Eric, though, was interested in making it easier for others to produce the kind of artwork that duplicated some of the mesmerizing landscapes he had seen. After meeting some other folks who could help, they decided to start a company. Looking for a name, they chose one based on one of these mesmerizing landscapes in the American southwest, Bryce Canyon. They felt that it represented the sense of wonder and beauty that can accompany such landscapes, and so decided to name the software "Bryce."

The software took a while to build and went through several versions before it really caught on. After a few years of struggle, it did catch on though, and eventually became a very well-known software product within the world of graphics and animation. Eventually it was bought by Corel and it is still a popular tool to this day.

This is a perfect example of a "bottom up" approach to business. It started with someone whose career path had led him, via a unique combination of his personal interests in geology, artwork and computers, to a vision of something special. This led him in turn to others who had been working on similar things, and with the mutual strengths, they eventually created a piece of software that became an acknowledged leader in its field.

More importantly, many users of the software, which is able to produce natural landscapes of incredible beauty, describe working with it as "an emotional experience."

The software, and the business, inspired a sense of loyalty that other companies can only dream of.

This is an example of a business that, although just as technology-oriented as the previous businesses I spoke about, had a *soul*. The overriding purpose for this product wasn't just to make money or to exploit a market trend—even though of course that is an objective of every business. The landscapes and life experiences of the creators "called" them to create this software, which was an act of creativity—of artistic self-expression in the same way that a painting or book is for an artist or an author.

Not Just for Entrepreneurs

I have seen many examples of businesses built from the bottom up, businesses with "soul" that not only went on to become very lucrative businesses for their founders, but have also become examples of superior products and service within their industries.

This concept of a "soul-less" business isn't just for entrepreneurs and venture capitalists. It applies to each of our lives, in our own careers, no matter what industry or profession we are in.

Consider a young adult who is deciding what field to go into, or what kind of job to search for. Imagine that the decision was made *only for money*—i.e. what job will pay me the most—without any regard for their personal calling, their likes or dislikes, or their strengths and weaknesses.

A job or career taken for the sole purpose of money is what I would call a "soul-less" career or job. Imagine someone deciding to become a doctor simply for external reasons—money, status, expectations of family and friends. They push themselves through college and medical school without fully understanding why they're doing it.

While this might seem like an absurd way to make decisions, it happens often enough. We would hope that only those who really have a strong inner motivation to help others and become healers would become doctors. Similarly for other professions, we would hope that there was some kind of calling.

The choice of career path is a big one. However, these days, with the average length of stay in a particular job decreasing, it is really a collection of smaller decisions that we make along the way that make up our career path. These small decisions, when taken together, combined with the circumstances that they were made in, weave the tapestry that becomes our career and life path—our personal Treasure Map.

A "soul-ful" job, on the other hand, is one that you've been led to by your own previous experiences and that somehow fulfills the "wishes of your soul." It is truly a collection of your "life experiences" to date, along with something new and fresh that can add to and perhaps lead to a different direction.

You can use your Book of Clues to help you make these little decisions along the way. Big Dreams, the "invisible hand" and other types of clues will lead you to the right place at the right time, as it led Eric, the creator of Bryce, to the talk on mathematical algorithms on his quest to build better images and landscapes.

CASE STUDY NO. 43:

Bryce Canyon, Redux

Speaking of Bryce, the software product, this brings us to an example of someone who was also in a time of transition. Claire, a successful web designer who was a little tired of designing corporate websites, wanted to do something new and fresh, but couldn't seem to decide what it was. She decided this would be a good time to travel, and though she investigated many places to which she might take a trip, for some reason, Utah kept calling to her.

This is an example of the "tickle": that little sensation you get when the "invisible hand" is pointing out something to you in your environment that might be important.

Meanwhile, she also felt called to start playing with 3D graphics, which she found more fun and creative than building websites. She found her way to a software package called Bryce, though she had no conscious idea it had been named after the landscapes in Utah.

She started to research on the internet where she should travel to in Utah. Salt Lake? Monument Valley? All of her research seemed to point to one area that she should visit: Bryce Canyon.

I was sitting with her discussing her upcoming trip and her quandary about what to do next in her career, when the discussion led to Bryce, the software. Somehow, we got on to the topic of how the software had been named, and she pulled out a book on the software. Of course, the book had on its cover a picture of Bryce Canyon.

It was an "aha!" moment in which she realized the synchronicity, the meaningful coincidence: that the software she had been exploring as she looked for an alternative career direction, Bryce, was named after the canyon she was currently planning a trip to visit!

This is a great example of how synchronicity "creeps" up on us without us even knowing it. We're often "led" by the "invisible hand" to two or more items, though there's no logical causal relationship between them; taken together, they form the kind of coincidental experiences we define as clues on our personal treasure hunt.

She took it as a confirmation that learning 3D graphics in general, and Bryce in particular, might have an impact on her future job prospects, even though she could think of no logical reason why this should be the case.

CASE STUDY NO. 44:
A Financial Storm and a Powerful Dream

Before we end, I want to share a powerful set of clues that I had during a tough time in my own career as an entrepreneur. Clues can inspire us, not just in the short term to solve some business problem or career issue, but also to help us find our broader purpose in life: our very own Treasure Map.

It was what we called a Nor'easter, a severe New England blizzard at the start of winter, and I could hear it starting outside.

I sat at my desk, alone in the first-floor suite of a shiny new office building in Cambridge, Massachusetts, just a few blocks from MIT, where I'd graduated a few years earlier. Anyone who would've seen me at the time could tell that I wasn't very happy—I had my head in my hands as I stared down at a few pieces of paper on the thick oak desk in front of me. It was our preliminary income statement for 1995—our second full year in operation.

I sighed. As the wind howled, I reflected on our early success—the *Boston Globe* had just featured us in its Business section, and our sales had grown to almost three times that of the previous year. In most industries, that kind of growth would have been cause for celebration. But the numbers in front of me told a different story. Our business plan, which I personally had sold to our investors with great bravado, called for us to grow fourfold, which meant that we had missed our target—in fact, we were almost *a million dollars short* of our goal. *And*, it meant that we had burned through almost all of our available cash, and were hemorrhaging what was left very quickly.

Something had gone wrong, and as I sat there, I began for the first time to doubt myself. Was I really ready for this kind of responsibility? The thought of all that we had built over the past few years going up in smoke was weighing heavily on my mind.

I walked home that evening (it was too dangerous to drive and I lived only a few blocks away), wondering what I should do, and how I should do it. I questioned whether I should remain the CEO of the company. Should I resign? Would it all come crashing down around me? I wondered if there was any way to turn things around.

That night and the next morning, I had several clues which pointed out directly where and how I should modify my business to get "back on track." It wasn't just about solving the current crisis in the short term; these clues led me to a whole different direction in my career—the direction of finding my purpose and calling in this life.

The first two clues came in a dream. In the dream, I saw that we as a company had lost our way, caught up in growth for the sake of growth. More importantly, I saw that not only had most companies lost their original purpose and vision, but most of the business world was suffering from the same ailment. In the dream I was on a bridge that connected the corporate world on the one side with a picture of us in the early days of our company on the other. The answer to our problems was to get in touch with the original soul and purpose of our business.

In the second clue, which happened in the state in between waking and sleep, I saw a vision of my old teacher meditating in the Himalayas and realized that there was a bridge between our careers (our "work" in this life) and our personal growth (our "purpose" in this life) that was often ignored. The way to bridge that gap was to get in touch with our own souls' purpose in this life through learning to follow our intuition and learning to follow the clues.

The third clue, which happened after I'd woken up, came in the form of a feeling. After several days of wavering and uncertainty about what to do, I woke up the morning after my dream with a strange feeling of certainty in my gut. This feeling itself was accompanied by both a *direct knowing* of what to do and *the energy to get it done*. I knew what I had to do to get the business on track, even though I knew it would be difficult. This feeling itself represented some sort of psychic energy that would be needed to get me through the short-term crisis.

My business was hemorrhaging cash, and there was no end in sight. The sales force had been making predictions that first my intuition, and then later the actual results, had shown were unrealistic. Tapping into both the energy and direct knowing, I ended up shifting resources to restore the company to financial health so that it was no longer in danger of dying. Over the next 90 days, I struggled with these decisions, argued with the management team I had spent so much time bringing on, and eventually got us back into a very stable place from which we could decide on the next steps.

While this was a short-term solution, this string of clues contained in the dream and the half-waking vision were part of a longer-term clue that came from a deeper part of myself. I knew that part of my purpose in life was to help not just entrepreneurs but people from all walks of life to get in touch with their passions but also with what they were meant to do in this life. The broader clue was about the business world in general: how it had become devoid of integrity, purpose and soul, and how to restore it through personal growth and seeking.

These clues, which happened many years ago, led me to write my first book, *Zen Entrepreneurship* and the current book, because of this urge to fulfill my own purpose in life, to follow my own clues to find my personal Treasure Map!

The Injection of Soul: Find the Treasure

The ability to use clues from the environment and from our dreams, messages from a greater part of ourselves, is an integral part of finding our own sense of *purpose*, *integrity* and *soul* in our careers.

To do this, we have to look beyond the simple-minded "dollars and cents" approach to our businesses, jobs and careers. Like many cultures before us, we have to find the thread that ties each of our personal hopes, abilities, fears and talents to those of the society around us. This can be done by learning to recognize our own clues and following our own Treasure Map to find the incredible future that awaits each of us.

Jung once said that the goal of therapy shouldn't just be to correct neuroses; it should be *individuation*. He defined this as the process of becoming the "person that you were meant to be." That's what finding the treasure is all about—finding and living your own personal destiny in this life.

If each of us does this, only then can we start to address the collective crisis of capitalism that we face today, bringing more integrity, purpose and soul to all of us.

That is the greatest treasure of all. Good hunting!

The Rules of Treasure Hunting

Here is a summary of the Rules of Treasure Hunting that have been presented throughout this book. If you have questions on any of these, please see the page on which the original rule appeared.

- TREASURE HUNTING RULE NO. 1: Pay attention to uncanny feelings (p. 36)
- TREASURE HUNTING RULE NO. 2: If it repeats, then it's most likely a clue (p. 39)
- TREASURE HUNTING RULE NO. 3: Clues are subjective, so every Book of Clues is personalized (p.51)
- TREASURE HUNTING RULE NO. 4: Apply the stages of the Clue Lifecycle to your clues (p. 64)
- TREASURE HUNTING RULE NO. 5: Clues usually indicate timing or direction, but rarely both (p. 74)
- TREASURE HUNTING RULE NO. 6: In every good hunt, one clue leads to the next (p. 89)
- TREASURE HUNTING RULE NO. 7: Sometimes a Big Clue will require no interpretation (p. 95)
- TREASURE HUNTING RULE NO. 8: Ignoring a Big Clue may prove futile (p. 100)
- TREASURE HUNTING RULE NO. 9: Pay attention when you have a Big Dream (p. 128)
- TREASURE HUNTING RULE NO. 10: Use the "keys" to unlock the symbols of everyday dreams (p. 154)

Acknowledgments

This book has been the culmination of my own personal treasure hunt, and many people provided "clues" along the way. While I can't possibly remember all of them, there are a few that I'd like to call out.

First, I'd like to thank many of my spiritual teachers and mentors, including Bill Kennedy, Andrea Seiver, Vyamus, James Forgy, Rama, the teachers at the Barbara Brennan School of Healing, and especially Robert Moss, whose teaching on shamanic dreamwork and synchronicity contributed greatly to my launching this project.

I'd like to thank the many wonderful people who contributed to the book through their stories and through many twists and turns. In that vein, I'd like to thank Lorin Beller, whose Big Fish group helped in spirit and in contributing stories, and Pamela and Joyce Latullipe, who encouraged my own search for synchronicity. I'd like to thank Susan Morgan and gera, both of whom encouraged this book to come together in their own ways, and Dannion Brinkley for his support and encouragement of spiritual capitalism.

A series of unlikely clues led this book on the path to publication, and I'd like to thank the folks in the Watkins orbit that were part of this path, including John Tintera, Michael Mann, Nick Fawcett, Slav Todorov, Jo Lal, and Etan Ilfeld. I'd also like to thank Wendy Keller who asked me, back in the 1990s what kind of book I'd *really* like to write, and I answered, "a book on synchronicity and business".

Most of all, I'd like to thank Ellen McDonough, not just for her support and encouragement through the many years that it took this book to come to fruition, but also, for being a key part of my own personal treasure hunt!

Notes

Chapter 9

[1] F. Greenwood, *Imagination in Dreams and Their Study* (London: Lane, 1894), p. 94.

[2] Robert L. Van de Castle, *Our Dreaming Mind* (New York: Ballantine Books, 1994), Paperback Edition, p. 6.

[3] Van de Castle, *Our Dreaming Mind*, p. 11.

[4] Van de Castle, *Our Dreaming Mind*, p. 23, and Jeremy Taylor, *Where People Fly and Water Runs Uphill* (New York: Warner Books, 1992), pp. 119–20.

[5] Van de Castle, *Our Dreaming Mind*, p. 24

[6] Taylor, *Where People Fly and Water Runs Uphill*, p. 29.

[7] Taylor, *Where People Fly and Water Runs Uphill*, pp. 29–30.

[8] From http://www.famousscientists.org/friedrich-august-kekule/

Chapter 10

[1] Dannion Brinkley, *Saved by the Light* (New York: HarperOne, 2008), p. 48.

[2] Brian Weiss, *Messages from the Masters* (New York: Warner Books, April 2001), p. 45.

[3] Michael Newton, *Journey of Souls* (St. Paul, MN: Llewellyn Publications, 1994), Second Revised Edition, p. 213.

[4] Newton, *Journey of Souls*, p. 249.

[5] Newton, *Journey of Souls*, p. 253.

[6] Newton, *Journey of Souls*, p. 257.

[7] SQuire Rushnell, *When God Winks at You* (Nashville, TN: Thomas Nelson, 2006), p. 3.

Chapter 11

[1] Fred Alan Wolf, *Parallel Universes: The Search for Other Worlds*, (New York: Simon & Schuster), p. 310.

[2] Wolf, *Parallel Universes*, p. 298.

[3] Wolf, *Parallel Universes*, p. 221.

[4] Paul Davies, *Other Worlds: Space, Superspace, and the Quantum Universe* (London: Penguin Books, 1990), p. 137.

Index

About the Author

Rizwan ("Riz") Virk is a successful hi-tech entrepreneur, angel investor, bestselling author, video-game industry pioneer, and independent film producer. Riz received a B.S. in Computer Science and Engineering from the Massachusetts Institute of Technology, and M.S. in Management from Stanford's Graduate School of Business.

Riz started his first company on a shoestring budget at the age of 23 and rapidly grew it into a multi-million-dollar operation with offices around the country and thousands of corporate customers. Since then, he has started, grown and sold several start-ups. Some of his hit games, which have been downloaded millions of times, include: *Tap Fish, Bingo Run, Penny Dreadful: Demimonde* and *Grimm: Cards of Fate.* He has also been an advisor, investor and mentor to dozens of other entrepreneurs and filmmakers.

Riz has produced many independent films, including *Turquoise Rose*, which was set primarily on the Navajo reservation; the online documentary phenomenon, *Thrive: What on Earth Will It Take?*, which has been viewed more than 70 million times; *Sirius*, one of the most successful crowd-funded documentaries of all time; and the cult classic *Knights of Badassdom*, starring Peter Dinklage and Summer Glau.

Riz's first book, *Zen Entrepreneurship: Walking the Path of the Career Warrior*, reached the top of Amazon's business and spiritual bestseller lists, and has inspired those seeking to integrate their work with a spiritual life.

His entrepreneurial exploits have been featured in *Inc. Magazine*, the *Boston Globe*, the *Wall Street Journal*, *Tech Crunch*, *Gamasutra* and *Venture Beat*, and were even skewered by the *Daily Show with Jon Stewart*. He speaks regularly on subjects such as start-ups, video games, meditation and career success, both in person and online on shows such as *Coast to Coast AM*.

Riz is currently managing partner at Bayview Labs (www.bayviewlabs.com) and executive director of Play Labs at MIT, a startup accelerator (www.playlabs.tv).

He lives in Mountain View, CA, and Cambridge, MA. To learn more, visit his website at www.zenentrepreneur.com.